To Dear Sasha
with much love

# COSMIC CONNECTIONS

GW00494559

# OTHER BOOKS BY MURRY HOPE

The Way of Cartouche
Practical Greek Magic
The Greek Tradition
Practical Celtic Magic
Practical Egyptian Magic
Practical Atlantean Magic
The Lion People
The Paschats and the Crystal People
The Psychology of Ritual
The Psychologyof Healing
Practical Techniques of Psychic Self-Defence
The Book of Talimantras
The Sirius Connection
Atlantis: Myth or Reality?
Essential Woman: Her Mystery, Her Power
Olympus: An Experience of Self-Discovery
Time: The Ultimate Energy
The Giaia Dialogues
The Nine Lives of Tyo

All Murry Hope's books are available from Thoth Publications. If you live in the U.K., and wish to recieve a catalogue, send two first class stamps and a self-addressed envelope to: Thoth Publications, 98 Ashby Road, Loughborough, Leicestershire, LE11 3AF, England. Tel 01509 210626.

Those who reside outside the U.K. please enclose U.S. $2.00 to offset the cost of international postage.

# COSMIC CONNECTIONS

## Murry Hope

THOTH PUBLICATIONS

ISBN 1 870450 20 5

Thoth Publications
98 Ashby Road
Loughborough
Leicestershire

Printed in England by Booksprint, Bristol

To all my beloved cats, past and present, who have helped to make my life on this planet bearable

# ACKNOWLEDGEMENTS

My gratitude and sincere thanks to Professor Peter Stewart, M.Sc., D.Sc., F. Eng., for a supply of current scientific information relative to my subject matter; Cynthia Kenyon, B.A., for invaluable assistance with editing; Christoper and Patricia Snelling for help with additional metaphysical material; Patricia B. Crossley, As.D., F.A.F.A., for permission to use astrological illustrations; Barbara Trueman, who provided the clue which served to fire my inspiration; and to all my students who have given me the confidence to write this book.

Additional artwork by Martin Jones.

# TABLE OF CONTENTS

# INTRODUCTION

Following the success of *The Gaia Dialogues*, and inspired by the work of astro-physicist Dr. John Gribbin, I was prompted to embark on a sequel involving the application of the 'field' theory to other cosmic bodies and their attendant intelligences. However, before effecting any judgments, the reader is strongly advised to consult the *Gaia* book, since it outlines the *modus operandi* employed in these excursions into the databanks of non-hominid consciousness, while also emphasizing the pitfalls involved. For example, before accepting the validity of any right-brain information obtained therefrom, the laws of science should first be applied, while a familiarity with the psychology of the Experimenter Effect, and the role played by the observer in quantum theory, is essential to the rational interpretation of any astronomical or astro-physical phenomena.

Since science is continually broadening our concepts of our relationship with the Universe, a radical change of attitude towards, and understanding of, forces superior to ourselves is therefore of paramount importance, our need to communicate therewith, both at the physical and subtle levels, becoming imperative. A cautionary approach is, however, advised, the Universal Consciousness being a wholeness comprised of different frequencies, mental access to many of which would appear to be decided by the wave-compatability factor and bandwidth of the prospective communicator, the overriding determinant being the cerebral program.

Although Earth may have provided the starting place for our somatic evolution as hominids, our fields, and the building blocks from which all matter originated, came from elsewhere in space and time. As astronomer Heather Couper remarked 'we are all the children of the stars'. It is therefore only natural that at some point in our evolutionary cycle we should seek to know more of our cosmic origins. One of the problems, however, lies in the fact that so much genuine paraphysical material appears couched in the terms of arcane iconography. This has proved a turn-off to many a scientific purist, as a consequence of which all new thought carrying a paraphysical emphasis is condemned out of hand. In my own case, having crept into the back door of astrophysics and quantum theory via the dark alleyway of parapsychology, I suppose I shall always be considered as something of a freak. But then England has always been known for its eccentrics, many of whom have contributed to the culture and ethos of our nation. For 'eccentric' try reading, '_free thinker_', one unfettered by the restrictive dogmas of the collective; and surely the best results from free thinkers come when they can dispense with hedonism and apply their creativity in disciplined modes.

So, while astrology will obviously be rearing its somewhat controversial head in the ensuing pages, it is by no means the primary feature, although the information I have uncovered during my researches has tended to emphasize the fact that there must have been a prehistoric civilization on this planet at some time in the past which was conversant with the knowledge possessed by modern science and much, much more. Plato's Atlantis, perhaps? But, since it is humankind's ultimate destiny to plumb the secrets of time-travel, I am happy to leave the answer to that one with the scientists of the future.

The ensuing pages lead the reader on a voyage of discovery into the mythological, scientific, metaphysical and parapsychological aspects of our solar system and the Universe which houses it. An attempt will be made to collate the various celestial energies with the chaos/order sequence, GUT (Grand Unified Theory) and TOE (Theory of Everything), the nature of and role played by Time as a personalized energy, and many other paraphysical/ metaphysical anomalies. And, finally, by effecting a combination of computer logic and the 'field' theory, (which I am given to understand is akin to the Eastern technique of _Samyama_ – from the Sanskrit 'fusion'), to instigate a series of dialogues with various celestial bodies and ultimately with the intelligence behind the Universe itself. A tall order, perhaps, but not in reality as daunting as it might sound.

So, let us forthwith 'set up a protocol' and seal it with the appropriate handshake!

Chapter 1

# THE GAIA SAGA

## THE 'FIELD' THEORY

For the benefit of those readers who are not acquainted with the contents of *The Gaia Dialogues* it is essential that I offer a brief explanation of the 'field' theory, via which I was able to devise a technique for accessing the databanks of the planetary genius to whom Professor Sir James Lovelock has accorded the name 'Gaia'. My intention is to extend this experiment further by effecting similar contacts with, and drawing information from, the fields of other celestial bodies, which is what this book is all about.

The premise is a simple one and can be condensed into a single sentence, *consciousness is a field of active particles begging organization.* From the layman's point of view this says very little, if anything, of the complexities involved. A more concise description might refer to it as a creative force or field, itself composed of many particles. And yet each particle utilized for conscious expression is in itself conscious, albeit to a lesser aware degree. Certain branches of science have recently become preoccupied with investigating consciousness and their discoveries to date are well documented in *The Gaia Dialogues.*

## THE ROLE OF THE BRAIN

But how does the field concept (or *Samyama* if you prefer), stand in relation to, say, the roles of the brain and certain genetic factors now known to exert specific influences on thought and behaviour? The electrical nature of the brain has now been firmly established and the nuts and bolts of its workings well documented. Dr. Susan Greenfield, speaking at the Royal Institution Christmas Lectures (1994), did an excellent job of putting some of this information into terms   more easily understood by the layman and, for those interested, this is available in illustrated book form from the BBC. Brains do generate electricity and, as Dr. Greenfield explained, although one cannot use that energy to run, say, a light bulb, these electrical impulses can be recorded and monitored. Neurons produce electrical signals each time they communicate with one another and the sum total of all the activity in the outer layer of the brain can be picked up by electrodes attached to the scalp. A machine called an electroencephalogram (EEG) translates this activity into a pattern of waves which are shown on a chart. These patterns may not explain what a person is thinking but they do give the experts a clue as to what they are *feeling*.

Dr. Greenfield tells us:

'The pathway from the highest level in the brain, the cortex, controls the fine movements you need for tasks like speaking and writing. The other four deal with semi-automatic kinds of movement you don't have to think about so much, including balance and coordination with sensory signals. All the movement systems work in parallel, each playing its own part but working in concert with others, and with the sensory system.

'Now that it is possible to build computers that do this kind of "parallel processing", we are beginning to understand how the brain manages this feat. But for a long time scientists had thought that there must be some part of the brain acting like the Captain of the bridge on the Starship Enterprise; plotting a course, receiving messages from passing craft, and sending instructions to the engine room. A hundred years or more of exploration through the universe inside our heads have failed to find it.'

So, while science is still unsure as to how, and by what, the brain is programmed, its role as an electrically generated computer places us firmly within the manipulative spectrum of at least one of four

Forces now acknowledged as constituting the Grand Unified Theory (GUT) or Theory of Everything (TOE) – electromagnetism, the weak and strong nuclear forces and gravity. A fifth, or 'reconciling' force has also been suggested, but scientists are still in the process of discovering, or establishing, what this might be. I propose it to be Time, and I am not alone in the concept that Time is an energy in its own right. My premise is based on the concept that matter, as energy manifest ($E = mc^2$), needs to enter a given time-band or slower frequency in order to effect that manifestation. In other words, matter/mass is time slowed down or waves becoming particles on being observed, non-local frequencies of time relating to the fuzzy world of non-locality in accordance with Heisenberg's 'Uncertainty Principle'. Dr. Lyall Watson once referred to time as 'a series of stationary bands through which we move' which would make sense in this context, although I daresay it will not be long before some far-sighted, open-minded physicist draws up a scale of Time's energies along similar lines to that of electromagnetism.

But to return to our brains and their programmers, the field theory provides a perfect answer. The field, or consciousness if you prefer, is a non-local component which exists separately from the brain and effects its programming via the electromagnetic web extant at the frequency of matter at which this planet operates. The soul or psyche could be seen as a more orthodox concept of the field but then, as with all fields, we are surely dealing with different bandwidths, while the brain itself is also dependent upon the societal software with which it has been programmed. Fields with extended bandwidths are capable of dispensing with this software and writing their own programs or, in terms of Jungian psychology, individuating from the collective.

Intelligence, therefore, may have little to do with field bandwidth (the evolution of the psyche, or soul age in metaphysics) thus a purportedly brilliant mind may be faced with the limitations of the field which will either manifest as blind prejudice, the inability to comprehend new ideas, or sheer fear of the kind encountered by those of strict religious belief when faced with evidence contrary to their tenets. Besides, intelligence is not a single variable, the evidence pointing to the fact that it is hierarchical (of a graded order) composed of different component skills which, for the sake of argument, are lumped together as 'intelligence'. Nor is it synonymous with either wisdom, intuition or creativity. For example, psychologists have noted that MENSA types with very high IQ often displayed low psi owing, no doubt, to rational (left brain) interference, while experimentation has also highlighted the lack of synonimity between creativity, psi, meditation and intuition, different brain-waves being employed for each specific function.

Other recent discoveries relating to how our brains affect our actions and personalities include the fact that the brain region that controls more action-orientated responses is more active in men, while the higher centre of the brain, which controls more emotional responses, is more active in women. Likewise the myths concerning the brain's decline in old age which, as we shall see later in this Chapter, has more to do with genetics than might have been thought previously.

The field is totally dependent on the brain for its imagery which, in turn, is dependent on the current program. In other words, there is a part of the brain which is designed for accessing non-locality but this is totally ineffective without the right software. In paraphysics (the currently favoured word for the more rational approach to metaphysics), the field (wave) only retains these brain-orchestrated images for a short period following separation from the body (particle) at death, unless the passing has resulted from a severe shock. Thus the program the brain carried from religious/cultural/educational sources leaves its imprint in non-locality until such times as it is wiped clean by a change in the field frequency. Therefore, people experiencing NDEs (near-death-experiences), and psychics claiming contact with spirits of the departed are, in accordance with the 'observer effect', likely to see only what they wish to see, or what they have been programmed to expect!

Scientists have recently been struck by the fact that in the part of the brain responsible for sight and conscious thought – the cortex – there are as many backward pathways as forward ones. According to Drs. Geoffrey Hinton, Peter Dayan, Brendan Frey and Radford Neal (published in *Science*, May 1995), these 'backward' connections generate dreams and fantasies to help train the brain to recognise images. The team modelled the forward and backward connections by wiring up two neural networks: one modelled the process that converts a picture into a representation in the brain; the second reproduced what goes on when the same picture is conjured up in the mind's eye. Both networks, it seems, can serve to train the other. These findings underline the importance of dreaming, a subject I shall be covering in a later chapter. Low cortex arousal, we are told, is disposed towards violence and lack of feeling for anything while high cortex arousal induces calmness, concentration, and a dislike of too much extraversial activity; the overall job of the cortex being to harness and rein-in the Limbic system.

Now I am no computer buff, my own word processor being elderly, to say the least, but I do find computer terminology rather apt when referring to cerebral activities, so I hope my readers will excuse my use of it from time to time. Here is a small example: when a piece of software fails to work as it should it is referred to as having an undocumented feature. In other words, it goes wrong when it is not supposed to for reasons nobody can yet fathom. And so it is with the brain, and that goes for *all* brains and not just those of the hominid species. Likewise, the bandwidth of our fields permitting, our brains may access the global/solar system Inter-net or even some cosmic Super-information Highway, which is precisely what I did with the Gaia Dialogues and, as I have already indicated, shall be doing with the other planets in our solar system and ultimately with the Universe herself! (* New information – see page 13)

## WIDER, MORE POWERFUL FIELDS

A TV programme on Channel 4 at 8 pm on 19th February, 1995 featured questions put to experts regarding the nature of the Big Bang and what actually preceded it. Some of the scientists interviewed admitted that they did not know, the question still being open to several theories, each of which begged the backing of empirical research. However, the Head of the Cerne Laboratories in Switzerland, famous for its particle accelerator, held a different view. When the question was put to him as to what existed prior to that tumultuous event he answered 'fields of potentiality', these being the blueprints of matter. In other words our Universe was guided to its birth by a superior intelligence which existed, among others of its kind, in a band of time way beyond our present comprehension. Or is it? After all, many of the great civilizations of the past were well aware of these powerful individuated fields of energy, but in order to render them comprehensible to the unlettered, their priesthoods or intelligentsia personalized them; they became the Neters of Egypt, the gods of the Sumerians, Greeks, Romans, the devas of Eastern belief, the Elohim or angels of the scriptures. They were the Old Ones, those beings who imprinted their archetypal influences across the pantheons of mythology, which Carl Jung, among others, saw as containing the encodement of the history of our planet from conception to conclusion. The blueprint was, in fact, well and truly etched, long before the advent of humankind.

From what I know myself, and what I have discussed with Gaia (who, incidentally, dislikes that appellation, preferring to be known as Danuih, which name I shall, in due deference to her wishes, employ from now on) these super-intelligences appear to be of different orders. For example, some are concerned with the manipulation of particles to create matter of the kind of which our Universe is composed, others with the provision of suitable physical habitats in which other orders of consciousness may experience. This principle, which deals with the 'manifest', has been observed by paraphysicists over the ages, its metaphysical connotations forming the basis of esoteric masonry (energy bound in matter, as symbolized in the masonic cord of Ptah). Doubtless this same principle applies at all levels and within all universes. And I firmly believe that our Universe, vast as it may seem as we view it from our limited perspective, is but one minuscule particle in an incomprehensible, timeless infinity; just as we are but minute particles of the body of Danuih, and the bacteria and other life-forms which rely on our bodies for their existence, are to us. A sobering thought, perhaps, but one which, as I see it, places us in a true, cosmic perspective. Science tells us that, prior to the Big Bang Time did not exist. But before either accepting or rejecting this premise it might behove us to see what the Universe herself has to say regarding her origins (see Chapter 13). Perhaps scientist and metaphysicist Itzhak Bentov had something after all when he coined the phrase 'The Universe is a machine for the distillation of consciousness.'[1]

## SLEEPER GENES, ALLELES AND MEMES

My initial experience in using the field theory to contact the intelligence that is the organizing force behind our planet was experimental. At that time I had little or no proof that the databanks

I was accessing were, indeed, those of Danuih, nor did I appear to have much backing from science as to whether the information I was drawing therefrom contained even the faintest grain of accuracy. The fault, however, was mine in that the limitations of my own software, in terms of reference, proved a real hindrance to her at times. However, since the publication of *The Gaia Dialogues*, evidence has been pouring in thick and fast. Here are a few examples.

When referring to the fact that she intends to shift her poles within the lifetimes of many of us, she referred to a 'sleeper' gene which some carry and others do not. This, she said, would become activated around the time of her shift, its task being to effect mutations in DNA which would initiate changes necessary for adaption to the new conditions worldwide resulting from the altered position of her axial rotation. This idea was, needless to say, greeted with more than a modicum of incredulity by the more rational among my acquaintances, and I confess to being dubious about it myself until someone pointed out the Biblical passage: 'The sun will be darkened, the moon will lose its brightness, the stars will fall from the sky and the powers of heaven will be shaken. Then of two men in the fields, one is taken, one is left; and of two women at the millstone grinding one is taken, one is left.' (Matthew 24, 38-39.) Surely there is no conceivable inundation, or cosmic fire, that would be so deliberately selective, but a gene would! In other words, we are pre-progrrammed genetically to survive or otherwise, that survival being dependent on our ability to adapt to the new climatic and other conditions with which we will be faced following the catastrophe.

And then science came to my aid in the form of a book by leading astro-physicist Dr. John Gribbin entitled *In The Beginning*, in which I was introduced to the allele. Gribbin tells us:

'Mutations do not happen suddenly, producing dramatic physical changes in the body of a new individual, compared with the bodies of its parents. Nor do mutations happen in response to environmental changes – the soft-bodied animals of the late precambrian did not "know" that it was getting colder, or that there were more predators about, and grow their shells in self-defence, rather, they must have carried an allele for thicker skin, competing with an allele for thinner skin. When the climate changed or predators spread across the seas, the thin-skinned individuals were killed, and only the possessors of the thick-skinned allele survived. Repetition of this process over many generations produced creatures with hard shells. [2]

But what exactly is an allele? Biologist Richard Dawkins describes these genes as *rivals* for the same slot on a chromosome the word allele being synonymous with rival. Dawkins writes:

'You cannot, of course, literally go and choose your genes from a pool of genes available to the whole population. At any given time all the genes are tied up inside individual survival machines. Our genes are doled out to us at conception, and there is nothing we can do about this. Nevertheless, there is a sense in which, in the long term, the genes of the population in general can be regarded as a *gene pool*. [3]

Interesting, no? Hidden genetic factors are obviously at work here to the effect that those life forms and individuals destined to survive a major quantum leap (pole-shift?) on a planet are preprogrammed accordingly, the 'sleeper-gene' or allele taking over and effecting the appropriate DNA mutations essential to survival, just as Danuih said (see *The Gaia Dialogues*). And are we not also being told that some scientifically unacceptable influence or 'field or energy' has already mapped out our future as individuals, and that of our species as a whole, no matter what Nature in the form of Danuih (Gaia) or any other extraterrestrial body might throw at us. Gribbin puts it this way:

'Taking a hypothetical example, even though the allele for blue eyes is recessive, it is widespread in the human population and may be present even in people with brown eyes. Suppose that some change in radiation from the Sun had made blue eyes an advantage when our ancestors depended on hunting and gathering to make a living. Then 'blue-eyes' would have spread very quickly – the 'brown-eyes' might die of starvation because they could no longer see well enough to hunt.'[4]

So, was Danuih's 'sleeper gene' really off course? Hardly. Any anomalies being due purely to the inadequacy of suitable reference material in my somewhat limited databanks. Interestingly enough, scientists studying longevity have discovered that evidence seems to endorse that it is a person's genetic make-up rather than lifestyle factors, as popularly believed, that holds the key to a long life, although this does not mean that lifestyle is irrelevant. Ann Kent, writing in *The Daily Mail Weekend*, Saturday 3rd June 1995, remarks that people who grew up in an age where they were forced to rely on their own immune systems for survival – antibiotics, modern screening programmes, diet and preventive medicines not being available – stood a better chance of living longer than many of us do today. She tells us:

'Research on centenarians has thrown up some rather odd findings. In France, where most people have brown eyes, scientists have found that the very elderly are likely to be blue-eyed...'

'There is no gene to identify a centenarian, in the way that there is a gene to identify someone with Down's syndrome. However, research suggests that centenarians are so-called supernormals, that is people with better natural body repair mechanisms than the rest of us.'

While on the subject of our planet being subjected to a possibly intensified field of short-wave radiation of the kind destructive to human and animal DNA, I am reminded of a question put to me in a recent lecture concerning the pollution of our oceans worldwide after the pole-shift, especially if the Moon (as has been suggested) should shift its position in relation to the Earth, thus affecting the tides. Gribbin comes to our aid yet again:

'... the trotosphere in which we live, and the stratosphere immediately above which acts as a lid to the trotosphere (because the warming layer stops convection, so that clouds and weather occur only in the trotosphere below) and shields us from ultra-violet. The crucial importance of this shield is clear from the fact that ultraviolet radiation is used as a sterilizing agent for surgical instruments, which have to be free of bacteria and other micro-organisms. The electromagnetic energy of this waveband is particularly disruptive to DNA – the "resonance" set up as DNA molecules absorb certain wavelengths of ultraviolet radiation is strong enough to damage the molecules. This is why solar ultraviolet radiation is implicated in skin cancer, which is a result of mistakes in cell division and growth produced by faulty DNA replication. The DNA of the earliest life-forms, lacking a thick skin, would have been particularly susceptible to this kind of disruption, so that life had to develop first in the sea (which, in any case, is where all organic molecules were dissolved). Perhaps a thick-shelled creature of the shallow waters, impervious to ultraviolet, might eventually have colonized the land, although it would have found nothing to eat there; but once the ozone layer was established the hazard was removed and relatively thin skinned plants were able to spread onto the land, to be followed by animal life.'[5]

What could be a better method of cleaning the oceans of the Earth than to submit the whole planet to an intense dose of UV energies? The end of life for hominids? Never! Rest assured that the alleles will have well and truly done their work by then to the extent that the survivors would not only be unaffected healthwise by the new frequencies encountered, but would actually *thrive* on them.

And I now add my (or rather Danuih's) piece in saying that, were her body (our Earth) to be moved slightly nearer the Sun so that over-exposure to UV and other harmful rays from the short-band range would play havoc with our immune systems, those of us carrying the convenient allele would not only survive this change *but also thrive on it*! Perhaps this process has already started. A photograph which appeared in *The Daily Mail*, May 8, 1995 showed a red frog, its fiery pigment believed to have been caused by physiological changes triggered because of extra ultra-violet light entering the atmosphere through the hole in the ozone layer. It is being studied by experts at Drayton Manor Park Zoo, Tamworth, Staffordshire.

However, it seems that alleles are not the only genetic factor at work in the background. Dawkins introduced the concept of memes as far back as 1976 when his book *The Selfish Gene* was first published. He writes:

'I think that a new kind of replicator has recently emerged on this very planet. It is staring us in the face. It is still in its infancy, still drifting clumsily about in its primeval soup, but already it is achieving evolutionary change at a rate that leaves the old gene (DNA) panting far behind.

'The new soup is the soup of human culture. We need a name for the new replicator, a noun that conveys the idea of a unit of cultural transmission, or a unit of *imitation.* "Mimeme" comes from a suitable Greek root, but I want a monosyllable that sounds a bit like "gene". I hope my classicist friends will forgive me if I abbreviate mimeme to *meme.* If it is any consolation, it could alternatively be thought of as being related to "memory", or to the French word *même.* It should be pronounced to rhyme with "cream". [6]

The influence of genes is further emphasized by recent research into PsychoNeuroImmunology (PNI), which has shown that many activities of the body take place through the communication between one cell and another without necessary input from the brain. In fact, some genetic factors actually appear to work against the brain. The tension set up by these conflicts of interest and intent which frequently occur between field requirements, genetic factors and cerebral programming are responsible for most illness and disease. Psycho-kinetic energies (PK), on the other hand, are emitted from the brain at a subconscious level, and can either attract or repel. For those interested, these unconsciously manipulated manifestations of PK have been well documented by Professor Stephen Braude in his book *The Limits of Influence.* PK potential would appear to be a property of the field rather than the genes or brain, although it obviously requires cerebral or genetic assistance to effect manifestation.

It would appear that we are entering a period of dramatic evolutionary changes during which some of us, like the man and woman in the Biblical text, will perish while others will survive to go from strength to strength. Fire, water, war, famine or pestilence, none of these will be pointing the finger of condemnation. Our fate will be decided by a certain preprogrammed genetic factor, orchestrated from a combination of the individual fields of those concerned under the direction of 'higher intelligences'. And so it is with the planet from whose body we derive our existence and the Universe as a whole.

The whole process of evolution, at all known levels and those beyond our present comprehension, is being stage-managed by

fields of consciousness we have yet to identify and understand. No
longer is it a question of simply effecting mutations at the physical
level appropriate to quantum leaps to be experienced by celestial
bodies such as our Earth, but also adjusting the program in the
cerebral computers of the retained species so that the survivors
actually understand, and quickly adjust psychologically to the new
level into which they have been catapulted by changes in the body
of their planetary host! Danuih was definitely correct in her
information; but then why should she not be since it is her body we
are talking about and we are, after all, no different in her eyes than
our own bacteria, and other minute life-forms to which our bodies
play hosts, are to us. As Gribbin so succinctly puts it:

> 'If the concept of Gaia means anything at all, then it is not too
> fanciful, some people argue, to extend the idea to regard
> humankind as a disease, infecting the planet and causing an
> unhealthy rise in temperature that will be detrimental to most
> other forms of life. Many of the people at the quasi-religious end
> of the spectrum of opinion about the Gaia hypothesis, though,
> regard Gaia as a comforting, mother Earth figure who will "look
> after us". They believe, on the basis of very slender (or non-
> existent) evidence that somehow natural processes will take the
> carbon dioxide we are pouring into the air out of circulation, and
> keep the temperature comfortable for people. But making life
> comfortable for the invader is not the way to get rid of a virus
> infecting your body. The fever that accompanies the illness may
> be unpleasant for a time, but it actually helps kill off the infection.
> It is only when the virus is disposed of that the body recovers its
> normal temperature. "People sometimes have the attitude that
> Gaia will look after us," Lovelock once commented to me, "but
> that's wrong. Gaia will look after herself. And the best way to do
> that might well be to get rid of us.!'[7]

Danuih's exact words. Perhaps we can see now why she was so
insistent that her slow rise in temperature is not purely the side-
effect of our industrial effluent!

Endnotes:

(1) Bentov, Itzhak. *A Cosmic Book*, p. 57.
(2) Gribbin, John. *In the Beginning*, p. 103.
(3) Dawkins, Richard. *The Selfish Gene*, p. 26.
(4) *Ibid*. Gribbin, pp. 103-104.
(5) *Ibid*. Gribbin, p. 99.
(6) *Ibid*. Dawkins, p. 192.
(7) *Ibid*. Gribbin, pp. 132-133.

\* Ref. from page 5

(Since I completed the manuscript of this book, scientists claim to have discovered a 'Time Machine' in the brain (the brain circuitry that controls our perception of time). By measuring brain activity as reflected by blood flow, scientists at Duke University, North Carolina, have shown that the brains motor control centre also keeps track of time, from milliseconds to minutes. Experiments show the striatum, a primitive part of the brain that was once thought to control only movment, to be resonsible for the computation of the time factor in the human experience).

# Chapter 2

## DANUIH'S RELATIVES

During my conversations with Danuih, she constantly referred to the other celestial bodies in our solar system as her 'family', and the Sun as her 'Mother', the latter for which I was obliged to produce some supporting evidence from the annals of history and mythology. Since the book was published I have had a chance to figure out a few of what appeared to me as either inconsistencies in the text, or statements which demanded a more rational explanation. Danuih being hampered by my concepts, I ended up laying the blame on the limitations of my cerebral software, the 'family' description being a prime example. A more logical (left-brain) approach might be to regard Danuih and the other planets in our solar system as having issued from the same cosmic mould, or linked system of particles, which ended up as those manifestations of mass/energy we see in our skies that are designated celestial bodies.

In order to view a rather large scenario such as our solar system with any degree of accuracy it is essential to draw away from it so that it assumes smaller contours which render analysis easier. This is precisely what I did and here are a few of my impressions, the first being more of a metaphysical nature. Consider a school as we know it, consisting of classrooms used by teachers specializing in different subjects. There is the science lab., art room, gym, etc. As pupils in this school we may find ourselves more in tune with one subject than another, or we may decide to opt out and play truant. But, as the story of the Labours of Hercules in Greek mythology is careful to point out, we must inevitably become proficient in all the subjects taught in that school before we are sufficiently qualified to be allowed to leave it and make our way into the great cosmic beyond.

Now let us put this into the planetary context. Each of the planets in our solar system has a lesson to teach all those life forms extant within the Sun's boundaries. These tutorial energies are emitted via the electromagnetic system and our brains therefore receive and react to them according to (a) our cerebral software, and (b) the greater or lesser megabyte capacity of our fields. In simple electrical terms, a five amp. plug, if subjected to a surge of power which it is not equipped to handle, will result in a blown fuse, or even a fire! All energy needs a terminal through which to express its value. Thus energy (information) is passed from universe to universe via a series of terminals and we, as people, are also terminals for the reception of energy/information from all cosmic sources. The amount of energy in the form of information we are capable of imbibing, however, is dependent upon the factors mentioned above. Likewise, since the molecular structure which comprises the mass of our bodies is literally frozen energy, the resonance of that matter or mass is contingent upon the receipt of energies compatible with its cohesion.

What is termed 'non-locality' by scientists, as applied to the fuzzy world of waves, can be viewed by the paraphysicist as the unmanifest, as against matter (mass) which is manifest, meaning it resonates at the same frequency as life here on Earth. Energies from non-local, or faster, frequencies cannot manifest at a denser level without a terminal at that level, in much the same way that electrical appliances need to be plugged in and switched on before we can appreciate their benefits. Similarly, information is being continually filtered through to the human brain from both non-local and recognized electromagnetic sources, faster frequency energies and those emitted from planetary intelligences, for example, being able to interpenetrate lower frequencies without the consciousness involved being necessarily aware of what is taking place; and therein we have the pattern of evolution so beloved of the Darwinists, evolutionary quantum leaps being inevitably orchestrated from faster-frequency fields or, as the esotericists would doubtlessly prefer, 'great beings of light'!

Much as the more sceptical among the scientific community may decry the idea, the planets in our solar system do exert an influence on us at *all* levels, and that means physically, mentally and fieldwise (spiritually to the more religious minded among my readers). Which brings us back full circle back to Danuih and Lovelock's *Gaia Hypothesis*, logic demanding that if Gaia is the self-regulating entity who can wipe out any life-forms on her surface which might prove a threat to her own development and well-being, then the same rule must surely apply to the other planets in our solar system, the galaxy as a corporate entity, and the Universe herself!

## DANUIH AND THE HOMINID COLLECTIVE UNCONSCIOUS

Each species extant here on Earth, or anywhere else in the Universe for that matter, has its own collective unconscious, which not only records the progress of evolvement experienced by that species, but also contains the blueprint for the entire cycle from beginning to end. The databanks of this collective unconscious are easily accessed by the planetary genius, a prime example of which may be evidenced in the way that Danuih reflects the thoughts and actions of hominids.

Details of a scientific survey carried out by I. Yanitsky at the Institute of Mineral Ores, USSR Academy of Sciences in Russia which was previously held secret, have now been released, and are reported on by Sergei Petrov in *Fountain Magazine*, No. 40, August 1994. These showed strange coincidences between the way people felt and the way the elements behaved. For example, the earthquake in Armenia was preceded by ethnic strife in the area, and the Romanian revolution was followed by an earthquake. Other examples cited by the author of the article, which appeared in *Literary Gazette*, included confirmatory incidences from Russian history which indicated a link between people's inner state and events in the life of the Earth. These findings, we are told, all seemed to suggest that local cataclysms and unrest were frequently followed by natural disasters.

Yanitsky's group, which had long been keeping track of such phenomena, noticed earlier that accidents and disasters were preceded by powerful destructive forces in the atmosphere, the Earth's crust, the hydrosphere and the gravitational, acoustic and helium fields. These processes affected not only man-made systems such as transport, communications, engineering structures but, most important of all, military arsenals and nuclear power plants. Petrov tells us that these processes, although invisible to the naked eye, were registered by instruments and became evident when the destructive energy erupted into natural calamity. This, Petrov felt, was not unlike a disease that afflicts the whole body, but only comes to the surface in the shape of an ulcer or a boil where the body is weakest. In trying to trace these destructive forces to their origin, scientists found that eruptions or negative emotions by large groups of people often act as a catalyst for devastating natural processes. The Earth, we are told, is definitely reacting to what is happening in the space around it and on its surface via the behaviour of people. The scientists concluded that the Earth's response appeared to be *intelligent and not merely mechanical.*

Yanitsky's studies confirmed what many have suspected all along: that the Earth is a living, intelligent entity, whose behaviour and feelings influence those species living upon her surface while she, herself, is also influenced by the goings-on among those life-forms for which her body serves as a school for cosmic growth and experience. There was lots, lots more in this article and, for those interested, the original material was published in *Inward Path* Magazine, 17/19 ul, Pravdy, 1235124, Moscow, Russia. Tel: (095) 213-7385. Fax. (095) 213-8474.

## THE CROP-CIRCLE PHENOMENON

But to return to nearer our own doorsteps, a consideration of Danuih's role in the crop-circle conundrum seems to fit in with this line of inquiry. Danuih obviously has access to the databanks of the hominid collective unconscious and as such would be conversant with the whole saga from the development of the species to the Ragnarok so vividly described in Norse mythology. Assuming, therefore, that someone as insignificant as yours truly can hold a conversation with her and, to a limited degree, access her databanks she, also, must both know and reflect what is occurring here on her surface. And, just as she must be extremely frustrated by the limitations of communication afforded by my scant knowledge, so she must find it difficult at times to get the message of what she intends to do over to humankind. The logical way would surely be to access the hominid collective unconscious for appropriate symbols, which she could imprint worldwide, that carry her message, albeit encoded in the mythology of the past, which is precisely what she is doing in the form of crop circles.

I have to confess that I am not a crop-circle follower. In fact, until one appeared in a field near to where I live I had tended to neither believe nor disbelieve in them. When I was taken to view this one, however, I changed my mind radically. My reason? Some weeks earlier, when on one of my 'cosmic probes', I was taken by the genius of the Universe through a timewarp (wormhole) into the future. I found myself looking down at Danuih in all her azure beauty while to the left there hung the rising crescent Moon. Suddenly, from a north-westerly direction (from my viewing point), a moving mass appeared in the sky, not dissimilar to the one which bombarded Jupiter in the summer of 1994. However, there was a distinctive feature in this one in that the centre, or largest fragment, looked just like an eye. It seemed to be heading straight for the Earth and I held my breath. However, well before the point of impact, it veered slightly to one side, hitting the Moon and knocking it out of its regular orbit around the Earth. This action seemed to produce immediate upheavals in the oceans of our planet, in much the same way that a bowl of water loses its centre of gravity if the surface upon which it is standing is suddenly shaken, or the angle of its support undergoes a radical change. These resultant oceanic upheavals caused the Earth to tip over what I roughly estimated to be some 90 degrees to the right (from where I was watching). And what relevance, you may ask, has this somewhat imaginative experience to do with crop-circles? The pattern of the crop-circle I visited *was exactly, to the last detail, what the Genius of the Universe had allowed me to view so clearly*. Now who is picking whose brains here? The picture etched out by the flattened stalks showed explicitly what I had witnessed earlier. There was the Earth, the Moon, and the approaching line of cosmic debris. Danuih is undoubttedly using images from the hominid collective unconscious via which to communicate her warnings: shapes and geometric designs which had meaning for our ancestors, the significance of which have paled in the light of modern technology and the materialistic society in which we are forced to live.

So, can any of us access Danuih's databanks? Some of us may think we do but there is only one way of finding out whether we are pursuing a reality or simply basking in the glory of self delusion; check your facts first and you will soon find out whether you qualify for the genuine experience. As may be observed in the 'psychic butterfly effect', like children whose choice of toys is swayed by the media – Ninja Turtles on year, Power Rangers the next – there are those supposed 'seekers' who are happy to flit from flower to flower, unable to progress beyond the gaudily-coloured information supplied by the seekers of quick cash. Like the discarded toys, all eventually end up on the rubbish-heap of human experience. Perhaps there is some truth in the jocular saying I first heard at psychology classes: 'The psycho-neurotic builds castles in the air, the psychotic lives in them and the psychologist (psychiatrist?) collects the rent!' One supposes, however, that soul-age (or field bandwidth) inevitably writes its very obvious signature on the personality, to be read with ease by those with the know-how.

So, when it comes to 'channelling' genuine information from so-termed 'higher sources' one of the deciding factors in the accuracy (or otherwise) of the content will be the updating of the appropriate cerebral software to accommodate the broader approach needed to comprehend and translate the thought patterns of a body such as a planet, unless we are content to bring through a load of rubbish! In other words, we must adjust our hailing frequency or suffer 'systems overload'!

The interpretation problem is further compounded by the fact that we have no specific terms of reference at present with which to evaluate right-brain (intuitive) promptings, especially those relating to abstract concepts, or information beyond present human knowledge. Researches carried out in the U.S.A. showed that the brain, when confronted by a series of abstract impressions with which it was totally unfamiliar (not accommodated by its software), tended to convert these into geometric designs. These designs were later found to be identical to those scratched on rocks by the Kalahari Bushmen in prehistoric times, and believed to have shamanic connotations. The average human brain, it seems, would be confronted by the same ring-pass-not!

I have heard many aspiring psychics complain that they never 'pick up anything'. Perhaps their minds are too cluttered with day-to-day events to allow space for right-brain communication. How can you receive a telephone call from a dear one if your line is constantly engaged? Over the years I encountered many so-termed 'mystics', who have gathered vast followings. But how many of these could survive the sort of tests to which I was subjected by Dr. Carl Sargent of Cambridge University in 1975 (under the auspices of the BBC). Although the experience was terrifying it was worth it, because it taught me to get my facts right by analyzing all right-brain impressions with left-brain logic. It also served as a sign-post toward the exacting and highly analytical path of paraphysics, via which I have come to know and understand the field theory. Unlike many of today's mystics and new-agers, in keeping with Picasso I do not seek, I find. Nor am I a 'psychic', or a 'medium' in that I am not manipulated by other fields, I simply access their databanks or whatever, while retaining full, conscious control of my own field, and complete awareness of myself as a discrete entity in my own right. However, since my information capacity is naturally limited by my software I am just as liable to error as the next person although my elemental origins give me a kick-start as far as contact with planetary bodies and other devic essences is concerned. Perhaps 'time-traveller' would be a better handle – if one must have one.


## OUR SOLAR SYSTEM

Astrology acknowledges ten celestial bodies within our solar system as playing important roles in the tides of human affairs, while also affecting the life-cycles of all other living things on the body of Danuih. These are: Sun, Moon, Mercury, Venus, Mars, Jupiter, Saturn, Uranus, Neptune, Pluto (see diagram).

Danuih, however, insists that there are two more, which have been accepted by some astrologers and even the occasional astronomer. The names generally used for these are Vulcan and Pan. The former lies close to the Sun and near to Mercury, and the latter beyond the orbit of Pluto. In a conversation I had with astronomer Patrick Moore, a noted sceptic, he assured me that he was a firm believer in the extra-Plutonian body, and anticipated a general acknowledgement of this in the not-too-distant future. Another scientist of distinction, mathematician and physicist Dr. Charles Musès, discusses the infra-Mercurial planet in his book *The Lion Path*. He tells us that the great astronomer Leverrier, who discovered Neptune, reckoned it to lie at a mean distance of 0.24

astronomical units (one such unit being the mean distance of Earth from the Sun) and to have a period of 43 days. Regarding Pan, he has this to say:

'Pan is the perturbationally indicated outermost planet of our solar system, with a perihelion just outside the aphelion of Pluto, that is, an orbit completely enclosing that of Pluto.'[1]

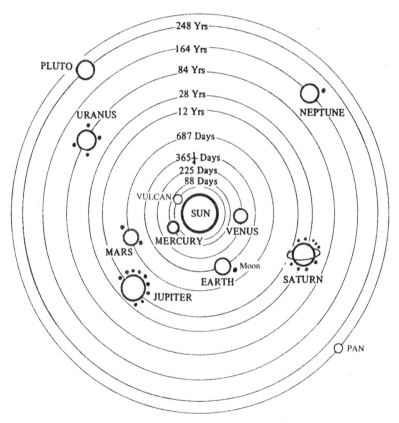

*Our Solar System showing the planets, their moons, distances from the sun, the length of their orbits and positions of two 'new' planets Vulcan and Pan.*

So, we have at least two scientists in agreement with Danuih's statement regarding the 2 additional planets.

The Sun and Moon are referred to by astrologers as 'the lights', and I confess to having problems with the latter. Danuih's insistence

that there were 12 planets, one for each of the zodiacal signs, plus
the Sun, would seem to indicate that she is counting the Moon as
a planet rather than a satellite. If so, then why not those moons
orbiting the other planets, which are generally viewed by astronomers
as being composed of debris left over after the formation of the solar
system? From what I have gathered from my researches, however,
it would appear that, unlike the moons of Jupiter, Mars, Neptune,
etc., our Moon was once a planet in its own right with an orbit
separate from that of the Earth. Proof? I have none, other than in
myth and legend, which abounds with information about a stage in
the Earth's history when there was no Moon as such; but, since I
have covered this subject in great detail in my books on Atlantis:
*Myth or Reality* (Penguin) and *Practical Atlantean Magic* (HarperCollins),
I would suggest that those wishing to pursue this line of inquiry
check therein for full details (and Bibliographical references in
other appropriate reading matter). According to Danuih, her
Moon was originally her 'partner', but therein lies another drama,
the end of which it would seem is set to be played out in the not too
distant future.


## A 'MOTHER' SUN?

The Solar Mother concept is by no means a new one. Many ancient
civilizations worshipped the Sun as a goddess. There were sun-
goddesses in the lands of Canaan, Anatolia, Australia, Arabia,
among Tutonic and Scandinavian peoples, the Eskimos, Japanese
and Khasis of India to take a few examples, several of these later
acquiring subordinate lunar brothers.[2]

It seems logical, however, to consider each of the planets as
having both an active and passive side to their natures or, as some
would prefer, a masculine and feminine or animus/anima. In the
Old Country (my term of endearment for Atlantis!), solar cycles
were acknowledged via the twin solar dieties, Helio and Heliona,
certain astrological 'ages' being sacred to either one or the other.
For example, during the zodiacal Age of Virgo, it was to Heliona
that homage was paid, while in the ensuing Leonian Age the
emphasis was on Helio. After all, our Moon has certainly changed
polarities during known historical times; in Egypt all the lunar gods
were masculine, likewise in Sumeria and several other parts of the

ancient world. It was only in the Matriarchal Age that the feminine emphasis came to be generally accepted. We shall have to see what 'Our Lady' has to say later in the book, I am hoping she will either confirm or deny recent scientific information regarding solar changes affecting the Earth. As I write this chapter, I have not yet commenced communication with the planetary genii; they may even choose to reject my attentions. Only time will tell.

## THE PLANETARY ROLE IN THE BIRTH OF JESUS

A recent column in one of the tabloids caught my eye as it related to the actual birth of the Founder of Christianity. Christmas, we are told, should be celebrated three months earlier if it is to mark the actual birth of Christ, research having confirmed that Jesus was born on 15th September in 7BC. Correcting the error would mean withdrawing the Roman calendar and 1993 would become 2000 overnight. One of the researchers, David Hughes, an astronomer at Sheffield University, examined contemporary astronomical records and pinpointed the appearance of the Star of Bethlehem to the rare conjunction of Jupiter and Saturn in Pisces in 7BC. This would appear to fit in with historical records, one reason Joseph and Mary left Nazareth for Bethlehem being to pay a tax which was levied by the Romans in 8BC.

Surely this information, which has been known to metaphysicists for centuries, puts paid to the 'end of millennium hysteria' so beloved of the prophets of doom? I find this kind of thinking ludicrous; but then what can one expect from a genus (hominid) which sees the Universe as revolving around itself, it being the galactic 'star-turn'! Australian physicist, Professor Paul Davies (winner of the 1995 Templeton Prize for Progress in Religion), in keeping with John Gribbin and Professor Lovelock, has a lot to say about this in his new book *The Mind of God: The Scientific Basis for a Rational World*. In an interview with Bill Broadway of *The Washington Post*, March 11, 1995, he stated:

'It has always been my position that the emergence of life and consciousness were not miracles, nor were they stupendously improbable accidents. They are part of the natural outworkings of the laws of physics. Of course, one of the tests of that hypothesis is that these same laws, which are universal, should work out the same basic processes throughout the Universe.'

Earth, therefore, has no exclusive claim on life forms that have minds and souls (consciousness or fields). Davies told his interviewer that contact with alien communities may be a long time coming, but powerful radio telescopes such as those being used in the new Phoenix Project in Australia can pick up signals from anywhere in the galaxy and may be closing the gap. As for UFO sightings, abductions, etc. he had this to say:

> 'It is extremely unlikely that interplanetary travel takes place. It is dangerous and expensive. Why bother to do it if you can exchange information using radio?'

Belief in UFOs, he states, like belief in angels, satisfies a need 'deeply rooted in the human psyche' that 'superior beings exist in the sky or beyond the sky which act as intermediaries to God'. He dismissed personal accounts of alien sightings and abductions, however sincerely given, as not being concrete evidence of extraterrestrial life. Which leads us nicely into my next theme, planetary intelligences.


## THE FIELDS OF THE PLANETARY GENII

Having established that there are twelve planets in our solar system our next port of call would seem to be the nature of these entities and, since there are also twelve signs of the Zodiac, whether the number 12 has any significance, esoteric or otherwise. I have suggested earlier that, following through the field theory, and the Gaia dialogues, each planet must obviously have a clearly definable identity via which to express its consciousness. In other words its sphere is its body and, like ourselves, it also has a soul or spirit. Just as we are all individuals, given to forms of expression exclusive to that uniqueness, so also are the planetary genii. Nor am I alone in this notion; the ancient Greek sages certainly contributed to the concept as I have outlined in *The Greek Tradition*.

The question I have been asked is, however, are these Intelligences synonymous with Jung's Archetypes, or are they simply manifestations of archetypal principles *as applied to our solar system*? I would suggest the latter, the Archetypal Worlds, as related to this Universe being, if one must put this into human terms, beyond the Universal perimeter. It seems obvious to me that there must be archetypes which in no way relate to our particular species or, in fact, to any genus extant on Earth or in the surrounding star-systems. Perhaps one day, when humankind has abandoned the slavery of the group-soul and individuated into a true cosmic awareness, these will become more apparent. But it would seem that humanity would require a greater understanding of other life forms *per se*, via which knowledge it could place its own standing into a corrective perspective, before such information would be made available.

Regarding the number 12 as mentioned earlier in this narrative I view this as relating to the Twelve Labours of Hercules, or humankind's need to traverse the experiences presented by the twelve signs of the Zodiac on the one hand, and learn the lessons given in *all twelve classrooms* in the solar-system school, before a release from the karmic wheel of Earth allows access via the closely guarded Gate of Hades (Pluto) out into the galaxy and from thence to the extremities of the Universe.

There are also a set of what have been termed 'Cosmic' or 'metaphysical' Laws, nine in number, which apply particularly to Earth, which I shall enumerate in Chapter 4, wherein I shall be dealing specifically with these aspects of our study. Anyway, those individuated fields who do have access to the Universal Super-Information Highway will know this already. But what does beg analysis as regards this solar system in particular is a knowledge of the workings of the planetary chaos/order balance, since this constitutes an important factor in human psychology and, in fact, the psychology of all life extant on the body of Danuih.

Endnotes:
(1) Musès, Charles, *The Lion Path*, p. 60.
(2) Hope, Murry. *The Gaia Dialogues*, p. 85.

# Chapter 3

# CHAOS/ORDER IN THE SOLAR SYSTEM

## CHAOS – A DEFINITION

The advent of the Chaos Theory heralded a new era in scientific thinking, works like James Gleick's book *Chaos: Making a New Science* (Heinemann 1988), and the Channel Four follow-up serving to alert the public to the fact that neither the seemingly unchanging laws propounded by eighteenth century science, or the previously favoured concept of nature as a capricious creature, were strictly accurate. Gleick quotes one physicist as saying: 'Relativity eliminated the Newtonian illusion of absolute space and time; quantum theory eliminated the Newtonian dream of a controllable measurement process and chaos eliminates the Laplacian fantasy of deterministic predictability.'[1]

The notions of prediction, or of a repeatable experiment, take on new aspects when viewed through the eyes of chaos. Things believed to be simple become complicated, and disturbing new questions have been raised regarding measurement, predictability, and the verification or falsification of theories. Nature is prolific in her spawning of irregularities, but the new mathematics of chaos have helped scientists to understand what is going on. It seems strange to me that no one had noticed previously how the immutable laws of Newtonian celestial mechanics, which dictate the monolithic regularity of the heavens, also produce erratic and unpredictable events such as the sudden movements of asteroids, comets and moons. Such knowledge has been known to metaphysicists since time immemorial but, without the proof demanded by modern standards of scholarship, it remained on the back-burner of knowledge, awaiting full circle for return.

However, more recent studies have tended to indicate that the truth lies somewhere in the middle, order and chaos being, in fact, somewhat cosy bedfellows! So it was only a question of time before science tumbled to the fact that chaos, like everything else in the Universe, has its natural life-span in that disordered systems can suddenly turn to order, which naturally gave rise to the concept of antichaos. Observance of this sequence, however, is by no means limited to the realms of physics and higher mathematics; it may be perceived in all walks of life, the history of the rise and fall of nations being a prime example. Order is often referred to in paraphysics as the child of chaos and likewise chaos is the child of order. It would be interesting to know how many geniuses have spawned children of equal mental stature and, likewise, in the arts and humanities. Since I am not in possession of any such statistics I am happy to remain tacit on that point and await the results of future surveys.

In the field of human experience, teenage is viewed as the stage when chaos inevitably accompanies change. This is followed by an orderly period which is believed to extend to the forties. Forty to sixty witnesses chaos, in the guise of entropy, slowly becoming more obvious, while from sixty onwards, although one is supposed to have settled into an orderly pattern of existence, chaotic elements are subtly accelerating towards the eventual demise when soma and field part company, the former eventually entering the natural recycling process.

There is, however, one interesting factor involved here in that both chaos and order undergo an acceleration process prior to the changeover. I watched this demonstrated on a computer graphic, where the simulated chaotic particles were accelerated to a stage at which they suddenly started to effect the change. There was one point in this simulation which struck me as being of significance, especially to the paraphysicist, and that was that the process commenced with one particle changing colour, followed by two others, the pattern assuming a triangular shape. Once this figure had been achieved, the rest followed suit with alacrity and order reigned. Are we being told that there is something in sacred geometry after all?

   The self-organizing nature of chaos, in addition to the inevitable decline of structurally ordered systems, was well known to the ancients, who chose to demonstrate their knowledge of the phenomenon by way of myth and legend. In Egypt, for example, there was the eternal combat between Horus (order) and Set (chaos) which was seen as taking place on a regular basis, the chaotic reign of the latter inevitably being overthrown by the eventual rise and challenge of the former. This story appears in many other myths, the Baldur/Loki episode in Norse mythology and the Lucifer/Mikaal encounter of Biblical note being typical examples. It is further exemplified in the ancient symbol of the caduceus (see illustration in Chapter 6), the two entwining serpents representing order and chaos respectively and the central pole the reconciling force. Is it not interesting that this has become the symbol of the healing profession down the ages? Someone in the days of antiquity must have been all too aware of the need for both these energies to be equally balanced in order to maintain a state of good health! Chaos, it seems, uncomfortable though it may be for many of us, is essential to the growth process in all life forms, from the tiniest particle to our own planet and the Universe itself. Without chaos all would stagnate while without order there would be no creation. Working on this basis does give us hope, mythology assuring us that the present reign of chaos, which even the most unaware amongst us must observe to be undergoing a process of rapid acceleration, can only lead to a long period of order – a Golden Age.

   The chaos/order sequence is also easily observable in the psychology of human behaviour while, to the student of life-cycles, its sequences may be seen to differ with each individual. These sometimes subtle, but also obvious, differences have been mapped out by astrologers in the sine-wave study of harmonics. If one takes a look at the lives of one's friends, acquaintances or working colleagues, it will soon become obvious that some enjoy longer periods of either order or chaos than others, while there are those for whom life seems to hand out everything on a plate for years on end, until the wave dips below the meridian into the chaotic, and then they wonder what has hit them! As one who suffers from the short-wave circuit, I have noted that although periods of order are often fleeting so, too, are those of chaos. This pattern has been observed to be less stressful overall than the former, especially where health is concerned, and probably gave birth to the old saying 'cracked crocks last the longest'!

There is lots, lots more that could be said about the chaos and antichaos theories in both science and paraphysics and how they manifest in areas as diverse as fluid dynamics, astronomy and genetics. From what little I have learned during my time travels it would seem that chaos and order close ranks with the evolution of the field or soul, as exemplified in the symbology of the triangle or pyramid. At the point at which order and chaos eventually fuse all time becomes one, perfect balance is achieved and the necessity for suffering thus alleviated. However, for the purpose of this narrative, my observation of these phenomena is mainly concerned with the chaotic or orderly nature of celestial bodies, from our humble Earth to the Universe itself, and how any changes in the functions and emissions of these essences affect us at all levels. Which brings us to an analysis of the chaotic or orderly inducing energies emitted by celestial bodies within our own solar system.

Many years of study have led me to conclude that, of the twelve planetary bodies mentioned earlier, six of these emit chaotic energies and six orderly energies. However, a word of warning. The fact that a planet, or anything, for that matter, is 'orderly', should not be taken to infer that it is 'good', 'nice', 'friendly', or any of those virtues in life that many of us feel to be desirable. Likewise, a planet emitting chaotic energies should not be automatically crowned with horns and fitted with cloven hooves and a forked tail! For within both chaos and order are the elements of both good and evil; it all depends on how we, as individuals, respond to those energies.

Since my dissertations on the chaos/order principle have caused some people to arrive at the erroneous conclusion that I do not believe in the existence of evil as currently understood, let us look at it in another way. While the evil side-effects of chaos are all too obvious such hardships can, in fact, serve to hone the spirit by inducing awareness which would not otherwise have developed. Excessive order, on the other hand, can produce a kind of evil which can limit the expansion of the field (evolution of the soul) by crushing the natural spirit of curiosity.

So, in the final analysis, we cannot blame the planets for our woes, nor can we justly accuse them of bringing about our downfall. Chaotic energies, for example, can be used to good effect to break down old and outdated modes and patterns of living; they can stimulate new ways of thinking and effect adaption to a more harmonious state of beingness, both personally and communally. Misused or misunderstood, however, they can lead to the stuff that hedonism, crime, riots, cruelty, mindless destruction, moral degeneration and the breakdown of society are made of. And, of course, they are inevitably conducive to self-destruction.

Orderly planetary energies, on the other hand, can make for harmony, better health, respect for all things, care of the Earth, stable living conditions and all those 'good' things that so many of us who belong to the older generation can see slipping away at a rate of knots. But such emissions can also bring about the kind of society which becomes so rigid that it inevitably stifles itself, chaos starts to penetrate the very roots of the culture it has so carefully built to the extent that its foundations begin to crumble and it inevitably collapses.

Fundamentalism is one of the blatant evils of excessive order, as it tends to stifle the expression of the creative/seeking aspect of the human psyche, while also condemning many less conscious life-forms to a miserable and terror-stricken existence. I find it interesting to observe how many people tend to place fundamentalism under the religious banner. I am sometimes tempted to think there are as many fundamentalists among the so-termed 'occult' and 'New Age' fraternities as there are religious fanatics. As I see it, anyone with a closed mind who adheres rigidly to one line of thought or belief, without giving even the slightest consideration to others, is either a fundamentalist or one in the making! This does not mean that I go along with the 'psychic butterfly' syndrome mentioned earlier, which borders on the chaotic extreme. Nor am I expecting the rest of the world to follow my own motto which is 'neither a leader nor a follower be'. After all, it has taken me light years of time travel to arrive at that conclusion and, in the final analysis, I could be wrong!

When taking an overall view of life on Earth, however, it is well to remember that like attracts like and, since Danuih is at present being subjected to a period of accelerating chaos (which includes a severe viral infection) during the period of lead-up to her pole shift, she is naturally attracting both negative energies and unevolved 'fields' (young souls) who have not as yet individuated from the hominid collective. As the pressure increases, such people are bound to exhibit chaotic tendencies at many levels. Only fields with extended bandwidths (old souls) will ride the storm, although not without some discomfort. Do not take my word for it; look around, read your papers, listen to your news bulletins; evidence of chaotic behaviour among so many, especially among the young, is there for all to see.

As my readers will shortly see, Danuih's basic nature is orderly, and she therefore dislikes intensely the chaotic mode into which she is at present being pitched by those universal forces which deem it necessary for her to effect a dramatic change. During the resulting quantum leap, she has made it quite clear that she intends to eject the invading virus, along with its adherents, in the not-too-distant future.

The overall effect of accelerated chaos inevitably leads to a resurgence of order, but within that acceleration lies the massive cosmic refining process that is set to produce the transformation necessary for the oncoming order sequence. Chaos has commenced to accelerate on Earth. Its effects, as has already been discussed, being obvious to all but the most insensitive. When the flames of the refiner's fire eventually engulf us as they most surely will, all those undesirable aspects of chaos will disappear as the energies unleashed effect their programmed mutations. Out of the cosmic window will go cruelty, hedonism, insensitivity, hatred, self-centredness, spiritual blindness, fundamentalism, and all those other 'evils' which constitute a threat to the seekers of a balanced order, together with their perpetrators.

So, what are these forces with which we are dealing and how do the planets and other celestial bodies feature in this unfolding cosmic drama? This is the point at which we take a deeper look at either the chaotic, or orderly, nature of Mother Sun's children, and the effects they are likely to have on our lives and the lives of all things extant on the body of Danuih.

## PLANETS OF CHAOS AND ORDER

Those planets emitting energies of a chaotic nature, be they for our good or otherwise, are as follows:

Mars, Pluto, Mercury, Uranus, Moon and Neptune.

And those celestial bodies whose emissions are more conducive to order and stability:

Pan, Jupiter, Saturn, Venus, Vulcan and, believe it or not, our own Earth.

One interesting discovery that has resulted from my researches into the natures of Danuih's family is that within, say, the chaos group of planets, two of these induce chaos at the physical/instinctive level, two at the psychological/rational level and two at the subtle/intuitive or non-local level which some might prefer to refer to as 'spiritual'. We are back to our triangular structure which could be seen to correspond, perhaps, to the hind, left and right compartments of the brain. Here are my results:

### PLANETS OF CHAOS

| *Physical/Instinctive* | *Psychological/Rational* | *Subtle/Intuitive* |
|---|---|---|
| Mars | Mercury | Moon |
| Pluto | Uranus | Neptune |

### PLANETS OF ORDER

| *Physical/Instinctive* | *Psychological/Rational* | *Subtle/Intuitive* |
|---|---|---|
| Earth | Jupiter | Venus |
| Pan | Saturn | Vulcan |

In the ensuing chapters I shall be considering the planetary energies in the light of astrology, astronomy, ancient arcane teachings and metaphysics which will, I hope, afford us a clearer picture of the forces with which we are dealing, alert us to the pitfalls, and show us how to make best use of them in all areas of life.

Endnotes:
(1)  Gleick, James. *Chaos: Making a New Science*, p. 6.

Chapter 4

# PLANETARY ESOTERICA

It would seem to be no coincidence that each of the planets has been named after an appropriate deity with whom its energies and attributes would appear to coincide. After all, the consciousness, or fields, of the planets themselves are considerably wider and more powerful than those of most astronomers and are therefore capable of both accessing the databanks of those who study them and implanting the appropriate information. No doubt this statement will be met with hoots of derision from classical scholars with astronomical leanings or callings who pride themselves on having effected nomenclatures appropriate to those planets' natures. Perhaps certain astronomers have, albeit unconsciously, drawn the correct information from those intuitive sources, the existence of which their rational discipline would not care to acknowledge. But in the final analysis does it really matter? After all, it is something of a chicken/egg situation if one cares to think about it.

## PSYCHOLOGY AND MYTHOLOGY

Many psychologists and psychiatrists, notably the great Carl Gustav Jung, have been quick to observe the relevancy of the myths to the human condition, and numerous books have been written pointing out the profound and accurate assessments of human psychology that lie disguised within the tales of gods, monsters, heroes, and those elements of nature consciousness that dominate the Classics in particular. And, bearing in mind the above references to those planetary energies which bear more than a vague resemblance to the immortals after whom they have been named, closer scrutiny reveals a definite pattern which indicates that the originators of these tales – if not those who actually recorded them centuries later – were fully aware of the deeper functions of the human mind. I also contend that, in addition to giving us a clear idea as to the evolutionary pattern of the field (soul), these myths also contain records of the past, present *and future* of humankind's sojourn on the body of Danuih. They are, in fact, outer-time (non-local) recordings of the collective unconscious of all those life-forms which have existed in the linear past and are destined to so do in the future, including the databanks of Danuih herself! I have covered the psychology of mythology in several of my own books, notably *Olympus: An Experience in Self Discovery*, *Essential Woman*, *The Psychology of Ritual*, *The Greek Tradition* and *Practical Greek Magic*.

Interestingly enough, Hercules' twelfth and final Labour consisted of fetching Cerberus from his subterranean portal to the world above and bringing him to the palace of Eurystheus as evidence of the fulfilment of his task, after which the hound was allowed to return to its chthonic domains. This, surely, tells all. The three heads of Cerberus, Guardian of the Gates of Hades (Gateway out of this solar system?) are the three earlier mentioned aspects of the self – the instinctive, rational and intuitive. Once the psyche has mastered/balanced these it is at liberty to pass out via the Kingdom of Hades (Pluto) into the wider Universe. In other words, it has individuated from the hominid collective and is ready to acknowledge, face up to, and negotiate myriad other life-forms within the galaxy and, perhaps, beyond!

## PLANETARY 'MAGIC'

My earlier studies of parapsychology led me along that path defined as 'magic', much of which I have since discarded in favour of a more paraphysical approach. Finding the best definitions in the semantics of science, I would therefore define magic/occultism thus:

A body of knowledge concerned with natural cosmic laws which, due to an overemphasis on the worlds of physical matter, has become severed from the scientific mainstream. So-termed 'occult' mysteries are therefore nothing more nor less than ancient scientific facts that have become encoded into terms of reference easily understood by the unlettered many of which, over the centuries, degenerated into superstition, their true meaning having been long since forgotten. Magic or occult energy works at three main levels:

1. The manipulation of particle aggregates (matter) via the agency of mind.

2. The conscious negotiation of particle/wave packets in non-locality (subtle energies on the 'inner planes' in popular magical parlance).

3. Imitating certain basic universal principles or patterns, which can have the effect of setting corresponding events into motion at the physical level, a process referred to as 'sympathetic magic'.

To these I would also like to add Rex Stanford's **PMIR** (Psi-Mediated Instrumental Response), in which he suggests that many of us are unconsciously using our magical powers to manipulate events to our advantage, hence there is no such thing as 'coincidence'. But now we are entering the world of parapsychology which, although obviously relevant to our subject matter, would require more explanation than I have space for in this book. Aside from all the mumbo-jumbo, however, the earliest and most sane definition of occultism I ever heard was 'a study of the Universe and all therein'; a far cry from the hocus-pocus that so many contemporary schools of magic have inherited from the Dark Ages. But then every man or woman to his or her own level, or so one supposes?

However, as the Principal of my old Alma Mater drummed into us first-year students 'it is unwise to throw out the baby with the bathwater'. The emergence of new lines of inquiry since my initial probings does not necessarily designate all earlier knowledge as invalid. So, before embarking on an analysis of individual planets, I would like to show my readers the table of planetary 'Rays', as I was taught them. Unscientific as these may seen at first glance, I hope to illustrate that my sources had at least some of it right, in spite of the much-maligned 'magical' tag!

## Table of Planetary Rays and Anti-Rays

| Planet | Anti-Ray | Stimulant |
|---|---|---|
| PAN<br>quickens, accentuates, heals via nature. | NEPTUNE<br>distracts<br>– diffuses, disperses, | MERCURY |
| NEPTUNE | PAN | VULCAN |
| VULCAN –<br>stills, masks, quietens. | MERCURY –<br>moves, communicates, heals by balancing. | NEPTUNE |
| MERCURY | VULCAN | PAN |
| MARS –<br>controls, directs, energises. | VENUS –<br>transmutes, harmonises. | URANUS |
| VENUS | MARS | EARTH |
| MOON –<br>negates, disguises, side-steps, reverses. | EARTH –<br>exposes, heals by sealing and binding. | JUPITER |
| EARTH | MOON | VENUS |
| URANUS –<br>splits, disintegrates.<br>(fission). | SATURN –<br>solidifies, weightens, (fusion). | MARS |
| SATURN | URANUS | PLUTO |
| PLUTO –<br>contracts, diminishes. | JUPITER –<br>expands, replenishes. | SATURN |
| JUPITER | PLUTO | MOON |

I was also taught to recognize planetary energies by their 'feel', the following list affording a few clues, although, of course, the degree of awareness would depend very much on the sensitivity or field bandwidth of the seeker.

JUPITER: A dull, fairly fast but heavy feeling.

URANUS: Sharp, erratic, difficult to hold.

VENUS: Light, fast, with a rhythmic undulation.

NEPTUNE: Vague, nebulous pulsations, difficult to either grasp or analyze.

PLUTO: A powerful, gushing, tornado-like whirlwind; beware the eye!

MERCURY: Light, airy, barely perceptible energies alternating regularly between orderly and chaotic modes.

SATURN: Tensive, cautious, bearing some similarity to Earth but slightly faster.

MARS: Very heavy, far more so than Earth.

PAN: Erratic, wispy and sharp. Lighter than Jupiter.

VULCAN: Fast, yet intense and solid, its energies carrying great impact.

EARTH: This is expressed in human terms for obvious reasons. Earth at present carries a dual influence, one aspect being emotional and kindly, the other cruel, hard and unsympathetic. Metaphysically, however, it should be functioning within a faster and more orderly frequency, which is why correction is needed.

MOON: Deceptive, stimulatory, confusing. In human terms similar to the negative side of Earth.

As I can clock up fifty or more years of practical metaphysical experience I feel entitled to state that the above table works at all three levels – the practical, psychological and subtle – while I have found the following list to represent a reasonably accurate, if not perfect, assessment of the energies emitted by our planetary neighbours. The ensuing chapters will, I trust, serve to show that all this is by no means as 'lunatic fringe' as might appear at first glance.


## OTHER PLANETARY ASSOCIATIONS

The astrologers of the past, many of whom, like Sir Isaac Newton, were also scientists of repute, associated each planet with a metal. Modern astrologers have followed suit and planets discovered in recent years have also received such allocations. My late guardian, a brilliant scholar whose discipline was chemistry, pointed out to me that the atomic weights of the different metals which, according to the ancient weavers of wisdom, came under the rulership of the planets, bear a curious relationship to the order of the planets and the days of the week. I do not doubt that certain metals, plants, or whatever, resonate more strongly to this or that planetary ray, but, as this is not my area of inquiry, such considerations are best left in the hands of those drawn thereto. However, for those interested, details as given by 'Sepharial' in his *Manual of Astrology* are shown opposite.

Of course this table covers only the seven with which the earlier astrologers dealt plus Sepharial's recent additions, so what of Vulcan and Pan and, indeed, Danuih herself? Well, there is a platinum (atomic number 78, atomic weight 196.09) which seems to fit into Sepharial's scale and might well suit Pan, while bronze, usually associated with the smithy gods, could possibly be allocated to Vulcan. However, bronze is actually an amalgam of various alloys of copper with or without tin and antimony, phosphorus, or other components, so I am happy to leave that in the hands of those more qualified to comment. Then there is the elusive, and as yet unproven, supposedly untarnishable orichalcum, so vividly described by Plato as the sacred metal of Atlantis. As we have no concrete evidence of its existence, let alone its atomic weight and, since Danuih's slow descent into chaos appears to have started with the Fall of Atlantis, I am inclined to allot this metal (if it ever existed!) to our dear Danuih, unless anyone has any better ideas?

## Planetary Metals

| | | |
|---|---|---|
| Pluto | Governs | plutonium. |
| Neptune | " | geranium and strontium. |
| Uranus | " | uranium |
| Saturn | " | lead |
| Jupiter | " | tin |
| Mars | " | iron |
| Sun | " | gold |
| Venus | " | copper |
| Mecury | " | quicksilver |
| Moon | " | silver |

The atomic weights of the different metals ruled over by the planets bear a curious relationship to the order of the planets and the days of the week. Thus—

| | | | | | |
|---|---|---|---|---|---|
| ♂ | rules | iron | .. | atomic weight | 56 |
| ♀ | " | copper | .. | " | 63 |
| ☽ | " | silver | .. | " | 108 |
| ♃ | " | tin | .. | " | 118 |
| ☉ | " | gold | .. | " | 196 |
| ☿ | " | mercury | .. | " | 200 |
| ♄ | " | lead | .. | " | 207 |

## THE ELEMENTAL KINGDOMS

Supplementary to the aforegoing are, of course, the elemental associations accorded by modern astrology which are as follows

Aries/Leo/Sagittarius –    Fire
Gemini/Libra/Aquarius –    Air
Cancer/Scorpio/Pisces –    Water
Taurus/Virgo/Capricorn –   Earth

In metaphysics these are believed to equate with the intuitive/creative/active; thinking/intellectual/rational; feeling/emotional/passive; and sensate/physical/practical aspects of the human psychological economy. Likewise with various other correspondences associated with the 'Primary Four' such as the

four taste sensations, the four 'humours', and music which, like
medicine, can also be divided into four main classes, a few of which
I have listed under:

|        | HUMOUR              | TASTE  | MUSIC /MEDICINE | SCRIPTURAL     |
|--------|---------------------|--------|-----------------|----------------|
| FIRE   | Sanguine*           | Sweet  | Stimulant       | Lion/Michael   |
| AIR    | Bilious* (Choleric) | Salt   | Tonic           | Eagle/Raphael  |
| WATER  | Phlegmatic          | Bitter | Narcotic        | Man/Gabriel    |
| EARTH  | Melancholic         | Sour   | Sedative        | Ox/Uriel       |

*In her book *The Four Elements*, Margaret Gullan-Whar reverses the
Fire/Air humour associations. Victorian scholarship being
renowned for its accuracy and depth of research, however, my
preference is for the Waite interpretation as shown above.[1]

For those interested in the deeper aspects of this line of thought,
a brilliant treatise on the Elements, their respective qualities and
their effect on the human condition, is covered in the work of Nancy
B. Watson, an accomplished magician, astrologer, numerologist
and student of Jungian psychology. Her book on the subject,
*Practical Solitary Magic*, is due out in 1996 (see Bibliography).

(Added later) While writing the final chapter of this book, and
during my dialogue with the genius of the Universe, she made it
known to me that there are actually five elements, as acknowledged
by certain Eastern schools of mystical belief. However, the fifth is
not the presupposed 'ether', but Time, Time Essences being, in
fact, elemental spirits from the same evolutionary stream as the
other four. But more about all that from the Universe herself (see
Chapter 13).

TIME

FIRE        AIR

EARTH        WATER

# THE ZODIAC AND THE GODS

The word 'zodiac', which actually means 'circle of animals', refers to a band of the celestial sphere extending about eight degrees to either side of the ecliptic, that represents the path of the principle planets, the Moon and the Sun. In astrology, this band is divided into 12 equal parts called signs of the zodiac, each 30 degrees wide, bearing the name of a constellation after which it was originally named but no longer coincides owing to the precession of equinoxes. Although thus described by most encyclopedias, from an astrological point of view this is not strictly correct and has led to many misconceptions and criticisms of its use in astrological analysis. The Zodiac is, in fact, a *conception* based on centuries of observation dating back 5000 years when it was supposedly devised by the Babylonians who noted that certain areas of the heavens appeared to emit specific energies which tended to effect distinguishing characteristic traits. Over the ensuing centuries various cultures have added their own imprints to the concept, sometimes allying the zodiacal signs to the gods of their own religions, a typical example of which appears in the work of Manilius (48 BC – 20 AD), who wrote:

> Pallas rules the woolly Ram and Venus guards the Bull,
> Apollo has the handsome Twins and Mercury the Crab.
> Jove, with the Mother of the Gods, himself is Leo's lord.
> The Virgin with her ear of corn to Ceres falls, the Scales
> To Vulcan's smithy, while to Mars the warlike Scorpion cleaves.
> The Hunter's human part Diana rules, but what's of horse
> Is ruled by Vesta with the straitened stars of Capricorn.
> Aquarius is Juno's sign as opposite to Jove,
> And Neptune owns the pair of Fish that in the heavens move.

As may be clearly seen here, the god natures of the old pantheon do not appear at first glance to equate with modern astrological interpretations. Or do they? Take a closer look: Athene ruling Aries, for example, which leaves the broody Mars to cope with the hidden passions of Scorpio. There are several other clues for the student to consider in the light of what we shall be discussing with, and about, our planetary neighbours concerning their zodiacal affiliations in the ensuing Chapters.

## THE HOUSES

The zodiacal circle is also divided into what are referred to as 'houses', each with its own specific influence as outlined under. An analysis of the planetary placings within these, plus the aspects effected between the planets themselves at the time of nativity, has constituted the basis of astrology over the centuries.

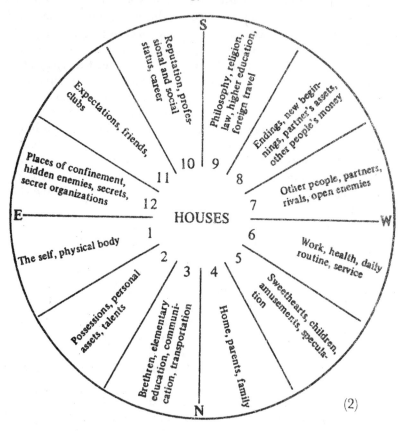

(2)

## COSMIC LAWS

And here, as promised earlier, is the list of The Nine Metaphysical or occult Laws which I am given to understand apply specifically to this planet:

## The Law of Rebound

This Law designates that a superior force will always cause a lesser power to recoil. To put this into more personal terms, if one comes up against another person, or a disembodied energy field that is stronger than one's own, whatever one projects in its direction will be returned PLUS the full force of the Rebounder.

## The Law of Three Requests

Rather more metaphysical, this one, in that it suggests that all requests which involve major decisions, be they related to matters material, psychological, or issuing from the subtle dimensions of non-locality, should be repeated in triplicate. The reason for this? The first utterance alters the conscious mind, the repeat engages the reasoning faculties while the third statement is believed to make direct contact with the psyche or field (as in the Biblical story of Peter's denial).

## The Law of Challenge

All visions, dreams, sources of inspiration, suspicions, anything, in fact, that would appear to issue from beyond the bounds of rational, logical thinking should be challenged. The lesson here is one of absolute honesty, as one should always be aware of the subtle line that divides the present reality from interpenetrative alien frequencies, and inspiration from delusion, the line between ecstasy and frenzy being indeed a fine one.

## The Law of Equalities

When two equal forces meet one will eventually give way to the other which then rises in status (increases field bandwidth or gathers mass?). This Law is re-echoed in the natural laws of science and may be clearly evidenced in particle physics.

## The Law of Balance or Equipoise

This Law designates that everything should function according to its relevant frequency or at its correct level. For example, sitting for hours round a table trying to drum up sufficient PK to move it six inches, when the same effect can be produced by giving it a slight push, is both a fruitless task and a sad case of misplaced energy. The Law of Balance is also concerned with the state of equipoise necessary for the satisfactory functioning and correct expression of energy at any level, which relates it particularly to the field of disease and healing. It denounces excesses of any kind and demands, for example, that the physical body be treated with courtesy because it is host to many other life forms including the four Elements, without whose kind offices there would be no molecular structure and therefore no physical body in the first place.

## The Law of Summons

Another more metaphysical (or parapsychological, perhaps?) Law, which designates how things do or do not respond to one's wishes. If, therefore, one makes a particular request, be it at any level, only to find that the response is either incorrect or disappointing, the fault may well lie within oneself. Either one is exceeding one's personal powers or requesting 'dues' to which one is not entitled. Such imposed limitations should not be blamed on so-termed 'superior forces' of either good or evil, as they may well originate in either the cerebral workings or the psychology of the person concerned. There is plenty of medical evidence to suggest that, when we want something badly, the brain actually goes into reverse and emits energies that either block or repel it. However, for the benefit of those among us whose paths have led us into non-local territories, this Law has more meaningful connotations, especially in the realms of exorcism, or the dispersion of negative force fields.

## The Law of Polarities

Positive/negative, anima/animus, masculine/feminine, active/passive, yin/yang – the process of individuation both rational and fieldwise – all these are expressions of this Law. We need to be well polarized within ourselves before we can tread the inter-Cosmic paths or, if you prefer, access the Cosmic Super-Highway. In faster frequencies polarity distinctions become blurred, the two aspects eventually blending into the One. We are advised that at our present stage of evolution the ideal state is for the anima and animus to be in perfect balance within the individual, neither obtruding or breaking cosmic law. But how many (if any!) of us are perfect! The answer is, of course, NONE!

## The Law of Cause and Effect

Commonly referred to among arcane teachings as The Law of Karma. But Karma is strictly an Eastern term although it is loosely used by many people to express the 'as ye sow so shall ye reap' principle. A generally unheeded aspect of this Law involves the exchange of energies, meaning that we should never expect anything for nothing, although the exchange need not always be in 'kind'. For example, a poor person receiving a gift of money need not repay in cash, but could render a service to the giver which is appropriate to their means and talents; likewise the rich person who inherits money he or she has not laboured to obtain. A simple, sincere thought, or prayer for another is often, by cosmic law, equal in energy output to the rich man's gift of thousands of pounds.

## The Law of Abundance
### (somtimes referred to as the Law of Opulence)

This Law expresses the attraction of like for like, e.g. money makes money, a fear is an unrequited wish, etc. My old Nanny used to have an appropriate saying, 'show me your friends and I'll tell you what you are'. As it was associated with non-conservation, in olden days it was referred to as 'The Miser's Dread'. When one is down to one's last penny or pound one is advised to go out and spend it, for an energy spent attracts a similar energy. I have frequently given away something I valued to a friend whose need I deemed greater than mine, only to find an article of similar type or value presented to me shortly afterwards. There is, however, a difference between throwing one's money away chaotically and expecting others to foot the bill and being genuinely in need through no fault of one's own. I often hear it said among esotericists that 'the Universe will provide'. I can assure my readers that she does, but only if one deserves it! Perhaps she will favour us by commenting on this phenomenon later in the book?

Although in the aforegoing I have tended to simplify matters by emphasizing the effect of these precepts on the individual, I do assure you that they can be applied to *all* levels of experience. How much of their message we choose to understand, or are willing to apply, will, however, be decided by such considerations as whether we are sufficiently open-minded to accord their possibilities an honest consideration, whether or not we have individuated from the hominid collective, and the bandwidth of our fields (soul-age). And thereupon I rest my case!

Endnotes:
(1)  Waite, A. E. *The Occult Sciences*, p. 44.
(2)  Crossley, Patricia. *Let's Learn Astrology*, p. 3.

Chapter 5

# PLANETS OF CHAOS, PART 1

## PLUTO AND MARS –
### *THE PHYSICAL/INSTINCTIVE EMPHASIS*

Having established in Chapter 3 that the planets in our solar system emitting chaotic energies are Pluto, Mars, Mercury, Uranus, Moon and Neptune, and that these can, in turn, be subdivided into those affecting us physically, psychologically, and subtly, analysis of the *modus operandi* of each group is called for. In other words, how their energies affect not only humankind but also all other life forms here on the body of Danuih.

As Mars and Pluto exert their strongest effects at the physical level it would seem logical to assume their energies have some influence over the lower chakras. For those readers who are unfamiliar with the chakras I would recommend *The Gaia Dialogues*, in which I have explained the system in some detail. But for the purpose of our present exercise we must needs move on to other, less familiar, territory if we are to cover the subject matter in hand. So, let us start with Pluto.

## PLUTO

**Astronomical Data:**
Viewed by science as the 'ninth' planet, Pluto was discovered in 1930 by the American astronomer Clyde Tombaugh (and purportedly named after Mickey Mouse's dog), although its position

had already been predicted by another American, Percival Lowell, who died in 1916. Irregularities in the movements of Uranus and Neptune indicated that they were being influenced by an invisible body. Strangely enough the agitator turned out to be surprisingly small; no more than 2320 kilometres (1,4440 miles), or one fifth of the diameter of Earth. It is believed to be made up of a mixture of ice and rock, with a surface temperature of 230 degrees C (-382 degrees F). Because it is not seen as massive enough to cause measurable effects upon its planetary neighbours, the planet that Lowell believed he had found may ultimately prove to be the elusive Pan, whose existence Patrick Moore is assured of.

Pluto has a much more eccentric orbit than those of the other planets. It takes 248 years to go round the Sun and, at its closest, it moves further in towards its fiery parent than the orbit of Neptune. So, between 1979 and 1999, Neptune rather than Pluto was/will be the outermost acknowledged planet. Pluto has one moon, Charon, which is one third the diameter of its host and moves round it every 6.3 days. Even through the world's largest telescopes Pluto looks nothing more than a dim star, and sensitive techniques are necessary to show both Pluto and his tiny moon.

**The Myth:**
I know I have said it all before, and in several of my other books, but I never cease to be amazed by the scientific accuracy behind mythology, Pluto being a prime example. The character of Pluto appears in the myths of many cultures, but mostly those which sprang from either direct contact with, or from folk-memories of The Old Country. He is the Hades of Greek mythology, also known as Pluto, from the Greek *plouton*, meaning wealth or riches, alluding to the treasures to be found deep within the Earth itself or the money to be made from the raw materials mined therefrom.

According to the legend, the three brothers, Zeus, Poseidon and Hades, decided among themselves, amicably, who should rule which territories. Zeus, generally accepted as the senior of the three, chose the sky, Poseidon chose the waters of the Earth, and Hades the Underworld, that place of darkness to which the souls of the dead were ferried by his faithful vassal, the Ferryman Charon. However, unless the deceased presented Charon with his *obolus*, he could not hope for his assistance which meant being stranded in a sort of no-man's land between life and death (time warp?). These murky regions were surrounded by the river Styx, while its portals were guarded by the three-headed monster-dog, Cerberus.

Pluto is seen to have a feminine aspect or anima in the character of the goddess Hecate whose attribute, a key with an unusually shaped top, combined the crossroads theme for which she is best known with the last phase of the Moon. Hecate, like Cerberus, is also often depicted with three heads.

Legend has it that once a soul has entered the kingdom of Hades it could never return to life, although there were always exceptions, the tale of Orpheus and Eurydice being a prime example. Also, not every person who died went to Hades. The souls of heroes, philosophers and those beloved by the gods were transported to the Elysian Fields, also known as 'The abodes of the Blest'. Among the ancient Greeks the exact location of these heavenly regions was debatable although it was agreed that they were not situated in the depths of the Earth. Some saw them as associated with a venue between the Moon and Sun, while others placed them way out in the Milky Way or in some far-flung part of the starry Universe.

**Astrology:**

Astrology tells us that Plutonian energies are concerned with elimination, renewal and regeneration. Underground activities are also laid at his doorstep, as are violent social eruptions, revolutions, and beginnings and endings. His nature has been likened to that of Mars in that his energies can be violent when released, and he has been allocated rulership of the zodiacal sign of Scorpio. Scorpio, as students of astrology well know, is associated with the deep unconscious and all things hidden or concealed, and at the physical level the sexual and reproductory organs. Pluto has something in common with Uranus in that his energies have a fission-like quality – they produce results by exploding outwards – unlike the cohesive fusion employed by the Sun.

Scorpio is one of the three signs allocated to the element of Water, the other two being Pisces and Cancer. Likewise the hominid deep unconscious and, indeed, the very essence of mankind. The ancients used elemental symbols to denote the true nature of certain species; the Lion always represented Fire; the Eagle, Air; the Ox or Bull, Earth; and the Man, – Water (see Chapter 4). As Danuih explained to me (see *The Gaia Dialogues*) her planet is composed predominantly of water, as are the bodies of hominids.

Water is the hominid element and therefore those planets most closely associated with that element are more likely to exert profound effects on the human condition.

## The Metaphysics:

My contention is that Pluto is the doorkeeper of this solar system in that he is the Timeway out of it; a kind of miniature Black Hole if you like. He is the ring-pass-not beyond which only those of appropriate field bandwidth may pass with ease. The dangers so strongly emphasized by those who believe Hades to be some sort of Hell lie not in being bound and tortured by demons, but rather by becoming *lost in time*. Therefore, to sell one's soul to the Devil, or Mephistopheles, means nothing more nor less than sacrificing one's uniqueness and spiritual freedom to another for gain. And that 'gain' need not necessarily be of a purely material nature such as wealth, or the fulfilment of physical desire; it could also be surrendering oneself to powers erroneously judged to be more spiritually advanced, with a view to partaking of what is seen at surface value as being 'great knowledge and wisdom'. True individuation requires the retaining of that discrete uniqueness that is the rightful heritage of all consciousness (fields or souls) *through one's own personal efforts*. The Greater Light is made up of innumerable *individual* particles, and one cannot attain to that state by forfeiting individual responsibility, via a free ride on the back of *some amorphous super-controller who dares to assume the nomenclature 'Master'*.

It was not without good reason that the Greek philosophers allocated the Helmet of Invisibility to Hades as his attribute. Hadean energies walk among us with ease; unseen, unfelt and unrecognized except by the wise who, unless they need them for some transformatory purpose, diligently avoid them.

In my study of the mythology of many races and cultures I continually encountered the dog/underworld theme. In addition to Hades' Cerberus there is the Egyptian Anubis, son of Nephthys, the 'Hidden One' or 'Concealer', also associated with that absence of light we call darkness and, reaching really further afield, the Eskimo goddess Sedna, who dwelt at the bottom of the ocean with her dog husband. There are many more examples for those with the time and interest to engage in research. The three heads of Cerberus doubtless allude to the triune nature of humankind; right, left and hindbrain in physiology; instinctive, rational and intuitive is psychology, etc., which need to be negotiated and balanced before the psyche can bypass Pluto and his Hound and speed on its cosmic journey to the Outer Time of non-locality. Surely, individuation from the hominid collective involves not only a balancing of the anima and animus within the personality, as Jung so wisely suggested, but also effecting essential mastery over that reconciling force which represents the centre line of the chaos/order sine-wave. So, chaotic though Pluto may be, his transformatory energies are essential to our development.

I am reminded of an incident which took place during Jung's travels in India. While visiting Konorak (Orissa), the great psychiatrist was shown a pagoda which was covered from base to pinnacle with explicit sexual sculptures. Seeing a group of young peasants admiring them, Jung took issue with his pundit regarding the possible dangers of the fantasy-inducing aspects of the display, to which the guide replied: 'But that is just the point. How can they ever become spiritualized if they do not first fulfil their karma? These admittedly obscene images are here for the very purpose of recalling to the people their dharma (law); otherwise these unconscious fellows might forget it.' As the two men continued their exploratory walk, the guide added: 'Naturally this does not apply to people like you and me, for we have attained to a level of consciousness which is above this sort of thing.' Well, dear Pluto, I think that says it all. So now it falls to me to effect a dialogue with you, if you will accept me, that is. For the benefit of those readers who are not familiar with the format I use in these communications, the 'M' is for Murry and the 'P' (or whatever, according to the communicator), for Pluto.

**The Dialogue:**

M: Pluto, may we exchange data, please?

P: Certainly. First of all may I correct a few misunderstandings concerning my role in what you described earlier as the solar-system school. Shall we say I teach geology and hydraulics? I think that is the best way of putting it although, of course, you must apply this to the human system as a whole, and not merely to the body of Danuih. Dredging is one of my specialities. I bring all the mud and filth to the surface (metaphorically speaking, of course), for unless it undergoes frequent airing it will deteriorate to such a degree that none of us teachers in this solar system will be able to help. It will need to be sent elsewhere to what your Crystal friends (and now, I notice, your scientists!) refer to as 'cosmic nurseries'!

M:   Is this the way in which you cause revolutions? If so, the blame for much suffering could be laid at your doorstep.

P:   Hatred, my little Time Essence, is always better out than in. The thoughts and feelings of those who perpetrate these acts of violence and cruelty are not *my* thoughts. My energies, as with all cosmic forces, are totally impersonal. Do bear that in mind. I have no axes to grind with either side in a hominid war or revolution, my role being solely to bring matters to a head. To use an analogy you yourself have employed so many times, electricity is an impersonal energy and, as such, it may be used to supply a hospital or to fire the 'electric chair' from which so many of your malcontents are frequently catapulted into my regions for corrective treatment.

M:   I was not aware that you specialized in correcting the hominid criminal fraternity.

P:   Correction is not the right word as it implies punishment of some kind in the way imagined by many hominids. When such a field ends up in my dark domains I simply effect a reasonable dredging job, and hope for the best. In other words, when faced with my specific energies, a field is forced to examine the deeper areas of its existence and why it has failed therein. These will be the basic emotions it experienced while inhabiting a hominid body, with the accent on its use or abuse of the lower chakras. But, please, refrain from associating me purely with sex and violence. After all, among the pupils that grace my subterranean classroom are to be found a goodly selection of financiers, while multi-millionaires are continually dropping in on me. Obsessions of any kind tend to attract my energies, while the purveyors of what you term 'fundamentalism' are usually equally divided between myself and Uranus, to whom the task falls of breaking down those patterns of extremity which have closed their minds so tightly and thus limited the expansion of their fields.

M:   You surprise me. I have to confess that I had never thought of
     you in this context. Tell me, how do you and Uranus decide
     who takes in who?

P:   We don't. Everything decides for itself, *according to the energies
     it emits at the time of death.* These personal energies are attracted
     to one or other of the planetary Teachers, who then do their
     best to correct the imbalances. However, the cosmic schooling
     of the hominid species is never easy, especially in your present
     time when Danuih herself is experiencing violent swings
     between order and chaos. Besides, the majority of beings,
     especially those still tightly enmeshed in the bonds of the
     hominid collective, pass over totally unaware of the *continued*
     existence of anything other than their own kind, let alone the
     interplay of planetary influences on their development.

M:   You have been associated with money and possessions, and
     yet one cannot help noticing that people who are rich are
     seldom generous, preferring to hoard their gains.

P:   You have answered the question for yourself. The misers
     inevitably end up in my domains for a goodly dose of
     'dredging'. You will not find any rich philanthropists among
     my pupils. The makers of money who have observed the Law
     of Non-Conservation, which you mentioned in your last
     Chapter, and spread their wealth around for the benefit of
     others, are more likely to end up in Jupiter's classroom than
     mine.

M:   Fundamentalists believe in a place called hell. Can you offer
     any explanation for this?

P:   Elementary, my dear Watson! (Did you know I was the patron
     planet of detectives or, for that matter, anyone who 'delves'?)
     If a person believes in hell then they will create that image
     which will persist in the field after death. And, since it falls to
     me to break the restricting bonds of false imagery, if they feel
     themselves to be 'sinners' they are more than likely to land on

my dark doorstep. I always enjoy a bit of mental fission; it clears the air for the field to receive a more constructive program. One of the first things I have to do when faced with such souls is to erase the image imposed upon the field by the software to which the brain has been subjected. As for a permanent hell, not guilty! No-one ever stays with me for very long, unless they want to, and then it falls to me to kick them out! All part of the fission-cum-dredging service.

M:    But you don't allow them to pass out of this solar system?

P:    Good gracious, no. If they are not ready to pass out by merit of their own increase in frequency then they will automatically return to Earth, their cycle of experience in this solar system being incomplete.

M:    So, what about those souls who, according to the ancient Greek beliefs, go to the Elysian Fields, or wherever. Why have they not passed your way?

P:    Because they didn't enter via my portals in the first place. Fields with wider bandwidths or, as some of your esotericists prefer to say, old souls from other parts of the Universe, naturally come and go via their original channels of ingress and egress. Let us take yourself, for example; you entered this Universe through a wormhole in the Sirius system, proceeding from thence, via The Mother, to Vulcan, and will therefore exit in the same way, stopping initially in the Paschat mode before taking leave of our Universe completely to reassume your Time role.

M:    Actually, I do remember the way in and out and have done so since childhood, but thanks for the confirmation; and does this apply to other beings who have come from other star systems?

P:    Well, that all depends on how and why they have come here in the first place. If they have come in the 'child' mode, in other words from another youthful planet, then they will need to pass through this Solar School before they can leave via my kind offices. And if they try to make a run for it Cerberus will catch them for me. Of course, I am making light of what really happens but you have my word that **no-one** leaves this solar system unless their energies are of a frequency which allows them to pass out directly via the refining fires of Vulcan. Remember, it is they who decide, not me. But, on the other hand, I will have my dues in terms of pupils. My alter-ego, Hecate, sees to much of this side of things for me. We each have our specific roles. She also effects Nemesis so, no matter how long someone or something may appear to get away with ill deeds, sooner or later she will be there at the proverbial crossroads of death waiting to collect them for me.

M:   It all sounds very gruesome and scary.

P:   In your heart of hearts you know better. The tales, legends and erroneous teachings of fundamentalist religions and restrictive regimes down the ages have etched their fearsome scenarios on the souls of mankind for too long. The time is fast approaching when all that mental celluloid is due for the disposal unit and I, as befits my personal mission, will be standing by to oblige. And upon that note I intend to sign off as I think you have endured sufficient of my energies for the time being. Your next port of call will be my brother, Mars. I wish you both a happy and instructive dialogue.

********

I have to confess that the above was not at all what I expected. One lives and learns. The genius addressing me has a great sense of humour. One could almost hear a belly-laugh in the background. Although he seems to enjoy giving the impression that he is being blunt I was more than aware of his hidden side, so well concealed by his mask of invisibility. Thank you, dear Pluto, for our interesting conversation but rest assured that, as an enemy of chaos, I am anything but deceived by the subtlety of your Helmet!

# MARS

## Astronomical Data;

Mars is much smaller than Earth, only about half the diameter, and is roughly half as far again from the Sun. In some ways it is more Earth-like than any other planet, with a day that lasts 24 hours 37 minutes and 23 seconds; it has similar seasons to those of Earth, although these are much longer because Mars takes 687 days to orbit the Sun. The Martian landscape is harsh; crated and rock-strewn and subject to violent dust storms. There are giant volcanoes, Olympus Mons being three times as high as Everest. It has no oceans although it has been suggested that certain craters were formed by massive floods. Freezing temperatures combined with a thin atmosphere produce icy fogs and clouds that vaporize in the day's heat and freeze again towards nightfall. It has two satellites, Phobos and Deimos (Fear and Fright), each of which is less than 30 kilometres (19 miles) across and unlikely to light up the Martian night.

For many years both scientists and science fiction writers questioned the possibility of life on Mars but recent probes have disproved many cherished theories. However, a stone from the red planet recently found its way into the frozen wastes of Antarctica and, although the discovery was made some years ago, the results of its analysis in the United States were not released until 20th March, 1995. So, what Martian secrets did this chunk of rock unfold? The presence of amino acids, the chemical building blocks of proteins, suggest that there was once life there.

Speculating as to whether the original Martians were hominid in type, science fiction writer Arthur G. Clarke, writing in the *Daily Mail*, March 21st, 1995, dismissed with disdain those sincere but deluded individuals who claim to have been visited by aliens. He commented:

> 'All their stories showed the same pathetic lack of imagination. Their alien visitors were invariably two-legged humanoids, with their bodies, heads, and even faces made after our own image.'

Bravo, sir. Danuih is with you all the way. He continued:

> 'That is too unlikely to believe. Life on Earth is astonishingly

varied; Life beyond Earth must be more different still. Here slime, mould, cockroaches, savannah grasses, giant squids, termite colonies and oak trees are all successful life forms. None have a body remotely like ours. We are the accidental product of millions of combinations of DNA molecules − far too many to be repeated by chance.'

While I cannot go along with the 'accidental' part of this comment, since I believe all fields to carry some intelligence quotient depending on their field bandwidths, the rest of Mr. Clarke's observations make sound sense.

So, what of all the fuss about what is believed to be a man-made face on Mars? For my part I would rather reserve judgment on that one until I have had a word with Mars himself.

**The Myth:**
Unlike Pluto, Mars is a comparatively simple archetype with which to deal. As with all other mythological war-lords Mars has his correspondences in most other pantheons. The Roman Mars was the Greek Ares, the Norse Tyr, the Anglo-Saxon Tiw, the Indian Mitra; and so forth. Patrons of war and battle often carry legal associations, which allies them at some point with Jupiter but, overall, their functions are obvious. Deities of the fight have existed since humankind first realized the need to defend their homes and possessions, but perhaps such divinities also have other, more caring functions; that is for us to find out. One interesting mythological point which emerges from the Greek tales is how the great Ares was defeated by the goddess Athene, the only warrior he was unable to conquer. Athene being 'head born' from Zeus indicates that her archetype represents a certain cerebral control which could be lacking in the Martian-type personality.

**Astrology:**
Energy, heat and activation are the keywords for Mars as given in Margaret Hone's *Modern Text Book of Astrology*. Positive Martian energies manifest in pioneering, construction, courage, energy, good leadership, passion and a high libido, whereas aggression, anger, destruction, impatience, pugnacity, foolhardiness, rudeness and over-emphasized sexuality come up on the negative side.

Mars is allotted rulership over the fiery sign of Aries, the Ram, which speaks for itself. The bright shade of red so often favoured by soldiers of the past crops up in all Martian activities. The ancient Egyptian priests, like their Atlantean colonists, realizing the stimulatory qualities of this colour, were careful to avoid it in all their priestly robes, preferring the calmer blues, greens, turquoises and whites.

Bearing all this in mind the two moons of Mars are aptly named Fear and Fright, the natural reaction to any display of martial aggression.

## The Metaphysics:

The gods of war are interesting in that the animus inevitably portrays all those macho traits in the males of certain species which are obnoxious to many of us, the tendency to depersonalize/dehumanize when absorbed into a group or collective situation being a prime example. But since I have already commented extensively on the psychology of collectives in several of my books, notably *The Psychology of Ritual*, I shall refrain from labouring the point.

Mars, or Ares if one is going to stay with the Greek archetype, could be seen to have a passive aspect, however, in the person of Athene, she alone who could fell the mighty warrior with a single stroke of her magic spear (the gift of Zeus – Justice?). The symbology employed here is obvious; her previously alluded to 'birth' when she leapt fully armed from the head of Zeus signifying the power of reason over instinct, or head ruling heart. What the myth is surely implying is that the passive/receptive aspect of the Ares/Mars archetype, although displaying the same strength physically as its alter-ego, is tempered by logic/reason which softens its reactions to provocation. Athene also excelled in the art of weaving, which suggests energies directed into more constructive/creative modes. Unlike Ares, Athene never really enjoyed battle, preferring to limit her energies to the protective mode. Hence her gift of wisdom, as depicted by her shamanic attribute, the Owl, while her protective aegis, which incorporated the head of the Gorgon, Medusa, demonstrated the role played by the mind in the overcoming of the id or lower self, as well as the additional strength of character to be gained therefrom. So, surely Mars has more to teach us than fighting, throwing our weight about and keeping our energies chained to below the belt?

I think this is the point at which I should ask him to speak for himself.

## The Dialogue:

M:  Genius of Mars, will you consider a dialogue with me?

MA: I see no reason why not. What would you have met tell you?

M:  In the Solar School, what subject do you teach?

A:  Physical education; the honing of the body in a disciplined fashion so that the negative side of my energies are put to constructive rather than destructive use and, in case you were not aware, I am also kindly disposed towards those who practise the art of surgery. As for war itself, my role in that arena is purely to supply the physical stamina such hostilities demand, the nuts-and-bolts side of modern warfare coming more under the influence of Uranus. As it is in the nature of my energies to produce physical effects, chaotic elements resulting from their misuse by any species on the body of Danuih is hardly my fault. Give a child an explosive weapon and, without discipline or instruction, it will destroy itself. I cannot be other than what I am, and it is not my fault that my rays are so often employed in the cruel game of war. After all, it is Pluto who starts wars, not me. I fuel them, but only through the misplaced loyalties and energies of those who fight them, either by choice or conscription. In truth it is about time that humankind grew up and stopped playing toy soldiers although, fortunately, this sickness is soon destined to be corrected, much to the relief of us all out here. Although Pluto and I work closely together at times, our functions are quite different. Your myths will tell you how the war gods were always friendly with the gods of the Underworld since they supplied the latter with a goodly amount of souls, the casualties of battle. However, in times ahead that myth will change. If I am supplying Pluto with any souls it will be purely for the purpose of instruction prior to leaving this solar system for good.

Let me defend myself by showing you my more positive

side or higher octave. Industry would be hard pressed without my help. My energies also encourage practical ingenuity. Although I am no architect, no building would be raised without the physical energy expended with my help. I also give stamina and the will to carry on against all odds. Take the case of those people who tire of life and all but end it until they suddenly notice a job that needs to be attended to – it could be something as simple as cleaning the house or mowing the lawn – but the energy thus expended can serve to throw cold water over their original plan, to the extent that they forego it in favour of more constructive avenues of 'escape'. Just one more small way in which physical expression, if properly used, can come to the rescue. Paschats, of course, were known throughout the galaxy for their supreme physical strength, which is one of the reasons why you feel so frustrated in a female hominid body.

M:   I know from my own experience that what you say is correct and I thank you for being so understanding as regards my personal, physical problem. And now may I ask how you will help Danuih in her forthcoming pole shift?

MA: By showing the survivors how to rebuild their world to make it a healthier and happier place, and to employ ingenuity in their new constructions, rather than brute force of the kind destined to cause them future illness. During the period immediately after the catastrophe, however, negative energies will run rampant but, as is often the case, the miscreants will end up killing off each other, the destined survivors being well out of the way and protected by Venus, Neptune and Mother Sun.

M:   It has been suggested by some Jungian-orientated friends of mine that the Athene archetype represents the passive/ receptive aspect of your nature. Is there any truth in this?

MA: It seems to amuse you to put these aspects into the mythological context. Fair enough; but, remember, these are only suppositions. I suppose you could say that the Athene archetype represents a more exalted aspect of my spiritual economy, although I must emphasize that we are not archetypal beings as such, we simply reflect the principles they represent.

M:  My friends will never speak to me again if I don't ask you about the face on Mars. According to astrophysicist Dr. Benjamin Frania, NASA analysts have privately concluded that 'far from being a natural formation as we once suspected, the stone face was almost certainly sculptured by human hands.' If this were the case, talent and skill obviously went into the construction of this mile long, 2,000 feet high stone monument. The assumption is that the stone face was modelled by our ancestors because the face looks like that of a human.

MA:  Why, oh why, do humans always think they are the only ones capable of creating such sculptures? I regret to inform you that your ancestors did not visit my surface and carve this effigy, and those among you who consider themselves 'advanced thinkers', who truly believe that civilizations of past hominids ventured forth into space along the technological lines you know at present, are sadly deluded. Yes, the image was carved, but not by hominids, or even by beings in their image and likeness. A small suggestion: are your scientists sure that the face is, in fact, that of an Earth hominid? I may not always share Pluto's sense of humour but on this one we both laugh heartily together. And now I perceive your stamina to be waning which means it is time to thank you for your company and acknowledgement of myself as a consciousness in my own right, with feelings and ethics. Call on me any time you are feeling tired, or need some help lifting or moving some heavy object; I will happily oblige.

M:  Thank you, Mars. I will take you up on that one. And thank you also for being so informative regarding your own role in the solar scheme of things.

********

A week or so after writing this an occasion did arise when I needed some extra muscle power to move a very heavy wardrobe which, try as I would, I was unable to shift. I closed my eyes and tuned in to

Mars and the result was phenomenal; with the minimum of effort on my part the object moved as if by magic!

Endnotes:
(1) *Memories, Dreams and Reflections*, C. B. Jung, p. 259.

Chapter 6

# PLANETS OF CHAOS, PART 2

## MERCURY AND URANUS –
### *THE PSYCHOLOGICAL/RATIONAL EMPHASIS*

Planetary energies affecting our mental attitudes tend to produce different effects from those conducive to physical reactions although, of course, it must always be remembered that the physical, mental, and subtle all form part of a threefold 'whole', each obviously affecting the other to a greater or lesser extent and which in turn interplay with the four elemental qualities highlighted in Chapter 4: the Intuitive, Thinking, Feeling and Sensate. However, compartmentalizing the influences may help healers and analysts to pinpoint the origins of a problem. For example, chaos caused in the physical system could well result in psychological stress and vice versa, while chaotic energies emitted from the field itself can produce an overall imbalance. Problems originating from, or accentuated by, short-term planetary transits such as those of the Moon or Mercury, are obviously less likely to last long whereas afflictions from the chaotic slow-movers need to be taken more seriously.

# MERCURY

## Astronomical Data:

The smallest acknowledged planet in our solar system (with the exception of Pluto) and, if one dismisses Vulcan, the one nearest the Sun. It has a sidereal period of revolution around the Sun of 88 days at a mean distance of 58 million kilometres (36 million miles), a mean radius of approximately 2 440 kilometres (1,516 miles) and a mass of 0.05 that of earth.

## The Myth:

Mercury is the Roman name for the Greek Hermes. However, as with all the major archetypal reflections, he has his correspondences in many other pantheons, notably the Egyptian Thoth, both having 'time' connotations. His main attribute, the caduceus, has been adopted as the insignia of the medical profession for centuries, although I doubt if many modern doctors truly understand its meaning. The caduceus features two serpents entwining the central, winged rod, one negative (chaotic) and the other positive (orderly), the central rod itself exemplifying the reconciling factor. The fact that the mind is capable of balancing these two forces is shown by the surmounting wings, which are believed to represent the higher or transpersonal self (field?), while the solar orb betokens the eventual return to some ultimate state of Oneness.

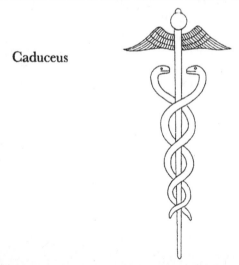

Caduceus

But the god Hermes was more than just a healer. He was also patron of travellers and herald to the gods, while all commercial transactions, diplomacy, learning abilities, communication, literary skills and adaptability were also ascribed to him. Likewise the reverse side of all these such as cunning, trickery, quackery, espionage, all crooked dealings, mental imbalance and communication problems.

**Astrology:**
Astrologically Mercury has always been associated with a person's mentality and type of nervous reactions. Communication, adaptability, logic, intelligence, versatility – all these are seen by astrologers as carrying the hallmarks of Mercury. Likewise, the negative aspects of each of these such as slyness, diffusion, criticism, double-dealing, loquacity, etc. He is said to govern the signs of Gemini and Virgo. The former I would agree with but, speaking as a Virgo, the typical Virgoan temperament and the Mercurian desire for constant movement and entertainment seem to have little in common. Vulcan energies are, as Danuih originally told me, far more in keeping with the Virgoan personality. Where we are all in agreement as far as Mercury is concerned, however, is in the duality of his nature which can be both endearing and dangerous. All Mercury's attributes and shortcomings suggest an airy rather than an earthy nature, so why is he always counted among those planets represented in astrology as a member of the 'earth' triplicity (the other two 'earthy' planets being Saturn and Venus)? One of life's enigmas that will, no doubt, be resolved during the planetary adjustments which are destined to take place at the time of or following immediately after the pole shift. Interestingly enough, the ancient Greeks associated Mercury with the sign of Cancer (see Chapter 4). Not without some good reason, no doubt, but perhaps the answer to that one lies in the far distant past when some physical representative of the Mercurial archetype first displayed his healing skills in the ancient land of Khemu during *the Age of Cancer*.

As Jung so wisely comments, the 'Mercurius' (Mercury, Thoth, Sîn, Hermes, Aion or any of the gods of Time) energies are neutral in that they are dualistic. So, although the chaos/order pendulum may be seen to swing with a degree of periodic regularity throughout the Universe, the way any 'essence' or 'intelligence' handles those energies at any given time would appear to bear some influence on its development as a unique entity or, as Jung would say, its individuation.

## The Metaphysics:

One must also include psychology under this heading, as Mercurian energies appear to have engaged the interest of many students of this discipline including one of the greatest of them all, Carl Gustav Jung. So intrigued, in fact, was Jung with Mercury, that he made a point of highlighting the close and mysterious relationship between the Mercurius, the planetary genius of Mercury, and Saturn, the Grim Reaper, both of which he felt shared certain influences related to Time and Chaos. He pointed out that in Gnosticism, Saturn is the highest Archon, the lion-headed Ildabaoth ('child of chaos'); but in alchemy the child of chaos is Mercurius. Jung commented:

> 'Mylius says that if Mercurius were to be purified, then Lucifer would fall from heaven. A contemporary marginal note in a seventeenth-century treatise in my possession explains the term sulphur, the masculine principle of Mercurius, as *diabolus*. If Mercury is not exactly the Evil One himself, he at least contains him – that is, he is morally neutral, good and evil, or as Kunrath says: "Good with good, evil with evil." His nature is more exactly defined, however, if one conceives him as a *process* that begins with evil and ends with good.'[1]

I agree with Jung that Saturn should not be identified with the chaotic elements in this solar system, the Gnostic concept probably originating in the confusion between the names 'Saturn' and 'Satan'. After all, Saturn was Cronus (time) to the Greeks; but more about him in Chapter 9.

Chaotic Messenger Mercury may well be, but surely one of his messages is that we heal ourselves by overcoming the chaos within, while we may also employ subconsciously the chaos of illness to effect either necessary psycho/subtle changes or, since we are all destined to leave this world sooner or later, as appropriate 'exit doors'.

## The Dialogue:

M: As you well know, Mercury, I am a little hesitant about approaching you, your reputation as a slippery customer having preceded you!

ME: Come now, the term 'slippery' is unkind, to say the least. May I suggest 'quicksilver' as a possible alternative? Besides, you have often benefited from my talents, loquacious though they may be.

M: If I am in your debt as regards help with speaking/lecturing, then I thank you. But the issues at the moment are hardly personal; they are more concerned with your specific role in the School that is this solar system.

ME: Quite, quite. I shall commence by defending my role. As is the case with all my planetary neighbours I do not spend my time instilling dual, or confusing energies into life on Earth. My purpose is to show two ways and which of those two ways people follow is their choice. Sadly, they often opt to try both at the same time, which results in the duality so often seen among those who lead double lives. As the hominid species evolves, its members will slowly learn to utilize my energies for balancing purposes or, as you would probably say, healing. As for my commercial associations, so often associated with crooked dealings and the like, the lesson I am trying to teach is the *balanced* exchange of energies. In an ideal society hominids would employ a barter system which would do away with the commercialism so rampant in your world today, the principle behind this being that, in order to obtain either wants or needs, energy has to be generated. In my book of cosmic rules, handouts accepted without this energy exchange automatically send the recipients to the bottom of my class. And unless they pass their Mercurian exams they do not stand a chance of progressing to the orderly class of Jupiter, wherein they would learn the correct way of gaining what they feel to be their just dues.

M: So, Mercury, you are telling me that, for example, the myth of your invention of the lyre, which you gave to Apollo in exchange for the caduceus (along with some sheep which were supposedly stolen from the Sun god in the first place) contains a lesson for us all. In other words the healing rays of the Sun are transmuted via your energies. But what about the sheep?

ME: Sheep are followers, are they not? If people choose to follow the ways of theft then they are using my exchange system in a negative way. It falls to me to highlight *both paths*. The choice as to which is followed, honesty or dishonesty, lies with the individual.

M:   My understanding of the myth was that it exemplified the natural powers of healing, as epitomized by the solar nature of Apollo, passing from the instinctive therapeutic mode to the logical and reasoning approach of clinical medicine.

ME: Also correct. But then humankind has taken that suggestion to the extreme, to the extent that the rational has been handed over to my associate, Uranus, to be dealt with at the altar of technology, at which humankind now sees fit to worship.

M:   Surely your healing association was, to an extent, also ignored by the ancient Greeks. After all, the Hippocratic Oath names such deities as Apollo and Asclepius, but there is no mention of yourself.

ME: The general tendency is for Teachers to hold their classes at given times. Over the entire period during which hominids have existed and will continue to exist on Earth, we teachers also have our periods of influence. Mine at present is more concerned with the practical aspects of hominid existence such as commerce and education, but there will come a time in the future when my balancing and bartering energies will come into their own; and that time is not all that far ahead. As for Herr Jung's comment on the *diabolus* of course I am not Lucifer, or any such being, imagined or otherwise. He is also correct in his summing up; my energies are impersonal. It is only how people use them that inclines them to either order or chaos or, as some might prefer to think of it, good or evil.

M:    What is your association with Time and the Egyptian Tehuti?

ME:   It will eventually fall to me to lead humankind into a consideration of the true nature of Time. This I will have to do via rational processes rather than intuitive promptings, although it could be argued that one inevitably results from the other. However, taking into consideration the climate of scientific opinion prevalent on Earth at present, such information is best introduced via those sources which are viewed as 'respectable, rational and logical'. But, relax, it will not always be that way. As for Tehuti, there was actually a person of this name whose medical and scientific knowledge gave birth to the legend. Tehuti and his family, all of whom were healers, went to Egypt from the Old Country (I like to use your term; I hope you do not mind?) during the Age of Cancer. Hence his association with that sign. Their deeds became the stuff of myth and legend. Tehuti was also a great recorder, having taken with him to the new country the history of the rise and precipitated fall of his own land. After all, any person incarnate on Earth, having attained to the necessary field bandwidth, is capable of reflecting the principle of an archetype, as I do myself. All of us planetary genii exemplify archetypal principles, but, as has already been explained to you, we *are not those archetypes*. The archetypal worlds are insubstantial in that, being waves rather than particles they exist in non-locality. Although I, like my planetary brethren, have my field or non-local aspect I also have a particle which is known to the peoples of Earth as the planet Mercury. Quicksilver, I might be, but even quicksilver has its uses, if you care to think about it.

M:    Astrologically you are given rulership over both the airy sign of Gemini and the earth sign of virgo. How come? Is your nature basically earthy or airy?

ME:   My influence is certainly strongest in the sign of Gemini. But then Gemini is, like myself, a dual sign. So your astrologers are in a sense correct. However, their surmise, although based on observation, is without logical foundation. My nature combines both air and earth, the former applying to my intellectual stimuli and the latter to my commercial emphasis. There is usually a teacher specializing in dual aspects of one kind or another in most planetary schools, balancing being the prime object of the exercise. Gemini is, as you well know, a sign of 'change' or 'crossroads' along the evolutionary path, in that those incarnating under its influence are usually faced with a choice: to proceed to a higher state of consciousness or employ my more commercial emphasis. Should they choose the latter, they will be obliged to return to my class again next term, and the next and the next if needs be! You could also view my dual aspects of air and earth in the active/passive context if you wish.

M:     Thank you, Mercury. I have learned a lot from our discussion. I shall consider your quicksilver aspects and how these can be best harnessed for the good of all. The word 'adaptability' comes to me. Am I on the right track?

ME:   Add 'acceptance and resilience' to make the triangle and the message becomes clear. Upon which note, I shall bid you adieu. Do feel free to call on me for all matters of literacy and communication but stay clear of commerce and gambling, these are not for you.

*******

URANUS

**Astronomical Data:**
Discovered by Herschel in 1781 Uranus was formerly named after him, as may be evidenced in the older Ephemerides, but was later renamed after the Greek god, Uranus, husband of Gaia. The seventh planet from the Sun, it revolves about the solar orb every 84.02 years at a distance of approximately 2 870 million kilometres (1,790,000,000 miles). It has an equatorial diameter of 51 800 kilometres (32,200 miles), a mass 14.6 times that of Earth, and five satellites. The most striking feature is its colour, which is greenish blue (most of the other planets appear as greyish or brownish except

Earth, which is an exquisite shade of blue). Uranus lies on its side and its winds blow in a retrograde direction, contrary to what is normal in the solar system. Voyager 2 discovered it to be covered not by glass as expected but by water. Although enshrouded by gases, below these there is an immense layer – 6,000 miles thick – of superheated water with a temperature as high as 8,000 degrees Fahrenheit. The rocky core is believed to produce radioactive elements responsible for the immense heat. There are also several other anomalies which would appear to form part and parcel of the erratic and disruptive nature attributed to this planet by astrologers.[2]

### The Myth:

Greek mythology supplies us with a detailed Creation Myth which includes a full account of the Uranian character. According to Hesiod, in the beginning there was Chaos, vast and dark. Then appeared Gaia, the deep-breasted Earth and, finally, Eros 'the love which softens hearts', whose fructifying influence would henceforth preside over the formation of beings and things. From Chaos were born Erebus and Night, who, uniting, gave birth in their turn to Ether, and Hemera, the day. On her part Gaia first bore Uranus, the sky crowned with stars 'whom she made her equal in grandeur, so that he entirely covered her'. Then she created the high mountains and Pontus, 'the sterile sea', with its harmonious waves.[3]

The Universe having been formed, all that remained was for the gods to people it, so Gaia united with her son, Uranus, and produced the first race, the Titans, of which there were twelve, six male and six female. However, she also gave birth to a host of other beings, the size, shape and appearance of which Uranus regarded with horror. So much did these ugly offspring offend him that, much to Gaia's horror, he shut them away in the depths of the Earth. At first she mourned their absence but her sorrow slowly gave way to anger and she planned a terrible revenge against her husband. From her bosom she drew forth gleaming steel which she fashioned into a sickle or *harpe* and, gathering her remaining children around her, she told them of her plan. All bar one were struck with horror and refused to have any part in the dastardly deed; only the astute Cronus, her last-born, volunteered to help her. So, when evening fell and the weary Uranus, accompanied by Night, retired to his wife's side, Cronus, who had lain in hiding in his mother's bedchamber, set upon his father and castrated him, casting the bleeding genitals into the sea. The black blood that dropped from the terrible wound duly seeded both earth and water, resulting in the births of the redoubtable Furies, monstrous giants, and the beautiful Aphrodite.

What we are basically dealing with here is a mythologized version of the events which took place following the creation of our planet, and the earliest experimental life-forms which graced her surface. Cronus is, of course, Time, to which, it would seem, the originators of the Greek myths, in common with the Egyptian sages, ascribed a specific personality. It has recently been suggested that the 'black blood' that fell from Uranus' wound equates with the dreaded 'black rain' which is believed to result from massive nuclear fall-out, and which would doubtless cause genetic mutations.

**Astrology:**

Revolutionary, disruptive, dictatorial are the keywords attributed to Uranus by Margaret Hone, while he is also known in esoteric astrology as 'The Great Awakener'. In recent years rulership over the Zodiacal sign of Aquarius, originally seen as the domain of Saturn, has been attributed to him, Uranian energies being far more in keeping with those qualities usually designated 'Aquarian'.

However, science and technology are not his only fields of activity, the more positive aspects of occultism have also been seen as falling under his aegis. Uranian energies stimulate originality, while those under his spell are often unconventional, inventive, reformative and outspoken. Negative traits, as might be expected, include eccentricity, rebelliousness, perversion, dubious metaphysical dealings and dangerous experiments.

**The Metaphysics:**

Unlike the gods of war with their emphasis on physical energy, as may be evidenced in the myth, the Uranian role in the cosmic scheme of things is somewhat more complicated, while the special relationship between Uranus and Danuih is highlighted. If we are to regard the myths as encompassing the complete life of Danuih, it would seem obvious that Uranus is somehow involved in any radical movements or changes that have occurred in her past or are likely to take place in her future.

In 1960 a German scientist, Professor Rudolph Tomaschek of Bavaria, stated that many of the people who died in the Agadir earthquake could have escaped had they been told by astronomers of the position of the planet Uranus, believed by many metaphysicists to be the oldest in this solar system. Uranus, he suggested, exerts a pull on the Earth's crust which acts as a trigger for manifestations of earthquake phenomena and Uranus was directly above the disaster zone at the time of the calamity. However, Professor Tomaschek's statement was hardly greeted with scientific acclaim when it appeared in that sober and responsible journal *Nature*, although his researches showed that, from a study of 134 great earthquakes he had made over a period of 49 years, at the time of 39 of these the planet Uranus was directly above the localities concerned. Many of his fellow scientists saw this as pure coincidence but, bearing in mind the myth and the erratic nature of Uranus, I am inclined to go along with Danuih, who refers to Uranus as her 'eccentric old uncle' and emphasizes his role in her anticipated pole shift, and keep an open mind. Perhaps my ensuing dialogue with him might serve to throw some light on the situation.

From my own experience Uranus's designation as The Great Awakener is valid. His energies, both at the practical and non-local levels, chaotic though they may be, produce results that are, more often than not, greatly to one's advantage. There are times when we all find ourselves in a rut. Nothing seems to move and, try as we will, we cannot seem to effect a break in the monotony of our existence. Then in steps 'Uncle' Uranus and wham, we find our lives turned suddenly upside down. And we protest. What became of that 'time of peace when nothing happened'? And yet, once the proverbial dust has settled and we have collected ourselves and reassessed the situation, the Sun suddenly seems to shine and we find ourselves all the better for the change.

Uranus and Saturn are strange, alchemical opposites in that Saturn restricts and solidifies while Uranus delights in breaking down or destabilizing old Saturnian moulds. Saturn can also contain Uranian energies should the need require. The fact that this metaphysical conundrum is played out in the alchemy of those metals appropriate to these two powerful players has always struck me as significant: modern technology uses lead caseings as a shield against the harmful rays of uranium while uranium, in turn, has contributed considerably to the nuclear power programme via the 'fission' principle.

As to this enigmatic planet's role in Danuih's and, therefore, our future, I am prepared to wait and see but, rest assured that, like the Biblical 'thief in the night', he will take us all by surprise and leave us with a better, cleaner and more balanced world.

## The Dialogue:

M:    'Uncle' Uranus, (If I may call you that since Danuih does!), I am a littler nervous about approaching you in case you do something drastic to my word processor, like causing a surge in the electrical current which is guaranteed to wipe my disk and undo my previous two-days' work.

U:    As if I would do that to you! Besides, you have just written about the *unexpected* way in which my energies operate, if you see what I mean? As for the 'uncle' appellation, if it amuses you I have no objection.

M:    Points taken. May I ask you about your influence over what we term 'technology', that is, the nuts and bolts of science rather than the more theoretical side?

U:    Who said I was not concerned with theoretical science? You have placed me in the psychological category as far as chaos is concerned which, surely, includes the theory of science as well as its more practical manifestations. I, like Mercury, work through human reasoning and logic, but I am also responsible for those sudden sparks of genius which bring radical changes to many things, not only on your planet but also in other parts of the solar system. Shall we say I am in the driver's seat?

M:    I thought that was the Sun's role?

U:    Let me put it this way; She invented the car which she allows me to drive which means she could, at any time, remove the vehicle. But for the time being I am her chauffeur. And may I pre-empt you on the subject of the negative/receptive aspects of my energies, the analysis of which appears to amuse you. As you well know we all have an active and passive side to our natures just as you do, one side usually predominating at any given time. If you must accord my 'other half' a mythological title, Urania will do nicely. After all, she is the Muse of Astronomy and her attributes are the celestial globe and compass!

M:   You know I am going to ask you this one – do you really have a role to play in Danuih's anticipated pole shift?

U:   And you know exactly how I am going to answer. After all, I am ruler of the Ascendant in your chart. However, for the benefit of those likely to read this book I will reply in the affirmative. But what I shall NOT tell you is how, why and when. One of the problems with hominid prophets is that their vision of future events is totally coloured by their software. Shall we say that, from where I am looking at the moment, there are very few whose software would accommodate the kind of information you are asking about. And this is a good thing. As you have said yourself, when I move it is without prior warning; in this statement I refer not to the idea that there is something awry with your planet at present, since that is common knowledge, but rather to the *modus operandi* to be employed in the carrying out of those readjustments necessary for the removal of Danuih's virus. Let me liken it to a proposed drama, for which production a special producer and director have been hired. Both these people may have a rough idea as to how they intend to present the drama but, as with all true artists, those little touches which dictate either genius or mundanity tend to occur during the process of production. Of course the play has already been cast, so those destined to take part in it are well aware of their roles and are busy studying their scripts, but the final result will, of course, depend on how deftly these are carried out. After all, we planets, like yourselves, are liable to error, although we are, perhaps, a little more conversant with the Laws of the Universe which we strive to observe to the best of our ability. I will say no more.

M:   I suppose that, given the nature of your energies and the sudden and unexpected way in which they tend to operate, I should not have expected finer details.

U:   Come, come; after all, your German Professor managed to
     penetrate my smoke-screen. Consider that I shall be entering
     the influence of Aquarius in January 1996, wherein I shall be
     in a position to use my energies in ways more compatible with
     my requirements. My sojourn in Saturn's mansion (Capricorn)
     has tended to keep me reined in whereas in Aquarius, as your
     equestrians would say, I shall have my head. So wait, watch,
     and be prepared. I have no more to say to you, so, be about
     your business with my blessing and I shall be about mine.

Endnotes:

(1)  C. G. Jung, *Alchemical Studies*, p. 228.
(2)  Sitchin, Z. *Genesis Revisited*, pp. 10-12.
(3)  *Larousse Encyclopedia of Mythology*, p. 89.

Chapter 7

## PLANETS OF CHAOS PART 3

## MOON AND NEPTUNE –
### *THE SUBTLE/INTUITIVE EMPHASIS*

Having examined the effects of chaotic energies emitted from those planets which would appear to influence life at the physical and psychological levels, the remaining angle of the triad, the subtle/intuitive, begs consideration.

Many pursuants of esoterica make the mistake of viewing all energies issuing from what they feel to be the subtle planes (I prefer non-locality!) as being 'spiritual', which could not be farther from the truth. Imbalances exist at *all* levels below the Infinite and, since I am highly dubious about hot lines to more exalted levels, preferring to believe that when it comes to contacting other dimensions we get what we deserve rather than what our egos feel us to be entitled to, we may encounter either chaotic or orderly responses or, as some might prefer, light or darkness. The growth factor lies in the recognition of our contacts, for better or worse, and how we handle their energies.

We have already discussed how chaos is a necessary ingredient in the balance needed for the continuance and evolvement of all life, so why stop at the physical? Science will confirm that there is as much, if not more, chaos in non-locality, as may be evidenced in Heisenberg's *Uncertainty Principle*, also called The Principle of Indeterminism, which reflects the inability to predict the future based on the past or the present. In quantum terms, it claims that one can 'never be exactly sure of both the position and velocity of a particle, the more accurately one knows one, the less accurately one can know the other'.[1] Eminent physicist Sir Arthur Eddington obviously saw both the truth and the funny side of this concept when he remarked 'something unknown is doing we don't know what'. Goodly advice for all students of the metaphysical and allied arts, which is also totally applicable to the nature and energies of the two celestial bodies we shall be considering in this chapter.


# MOON

**Astronomical Data:**
The Moon which lights our nights is the Earth's only satellite. It is also exceptionally large when compared to the satellites of other planets, which should tell us something to start with. Its obvious features have long been known: – it creates the tides, its phases mark its monthly orbit, it is scarred with craters and dark areas known as 'seas' (*maria*) and it keeps one side permanently towards the Earth. It is no longer maintained that the Earth and the Moon were originally one body, the satellite having always been separate from the Earth. Both are also believed to be about as old, the Moon having been formed some 4,600 million years ago. Many astronomers believe that its craters were formed by meteorite impacts more than 3,000 million years ago, very large strikes having caused molten rock to flow and form the *maria*. However, there is another school of astronomical thought which opines that volcanic activity played a major role in the moulding of the lunar surface, a rain of tiny particles having eroded the surface into a thin layer of dust. Space research between 1960 and 1975 revealed much more detail. The first manned mission to its surface, Apollo 11, landed in the Sea of Tranquillity, while Apollo 17, last of the lunar missions, landed on The Sea of Serenity in December 1972. Geologist Harrison Schmitt, who was one of the crew on this mission, discovered some 'orange soil': tiny glass beads formed by intense heat, together with other information which has proved valuable to scientific research.

But just how long has Earth really been saddled with this satellite? Mainstream science tends to stay with the orthodox view that our Moon has been around a long, long time, but not so all of its members. There is, for example, a school of thought which opines that our Moon was once a planet in its own right that became pulled into Earth's orbit following a series of astronomical disasters which ruined its surface. For those interested in this line of inquiry, full details are given in the writings of H. S. Bellamy, notably *Moons, Myths and Man*, in which he outlines the lunar theory put forward by the German astronomer/physicist Professor Hans Hoerbiger, in the 1930s, and more recently supported by a Frenchman, Professor Denis Saurat, in his book *Atlantis and the Giants*. Saurat proposed that the height of people is greatly influenced by the Moon's gravitational pull so, in days long past when, as the Scripture tell us, 'There were Giants in those days', this was due to the fact that *there was no Moon*. Being a man of erudition, Saurat supports his theory with plenty of evidence.

Certain esoteric schools of thought also subscribe to the idea that the Moon was once a planet in its own right (the Lucifer character in the Christo/Judaic Scriptures?) which, for some reason we may never know, was battered to near destruction by cosmic forces and sent hurling in our direction. Perhaps the cosmic bombardment to which the scientists tell us the orb was subjected was carried out via the agency of a Higher Force. Call that Force 'Mikaal' if it makes you happy, but my own feeling is that it is not as simple as that.

The idea of a moonless Earth raises many questions, not the least of which is how our planet would, or could, exist without the gravitational pull exerted by its satellite. An article which appeared in the 'Science Notebook' column of *The Washington Post* in 1993 had this to say:

'Aside from a dramatic decline in romance and werewolf activity what would life be on Earth without the moon? Very different at best and maybe impossible at worst, according to researchers from the Bureau des Longitudes in Paris.

'That is because the moon exercises a stabilizing influence on our planet's orientation in space, and hence its climate change.

'The Earth's predictable seasonal variation is determined by the fact that it is tilted 23 degrees from the perpendicular as it orbits the sun. (If it spun exactly perpendicular to its orbit, the maximum amount of sunlight would always hit the equator instead of alternating between northern and southern hemispheres.) So critical is the inclination that even tiny periodic variations of about 1 degree – which happen every few thousand years thanks to the fact that the Earth wobbles slightly as it spins – are believed to trigger ice ages.

'Astronomers call this tilt "obliquity", and it varies dramatically over time, J. Laskar and colleagues report in the current *Nature*. Using celestial data and mathematical models, they calculate that the obliquities of the inner planets of our solar system – and thus their climates – have fluctuated wildly in the past, and that of Mars is still changing.

' "This should probably be taken into consideration," the researchers write, "when estimating the probability of finding a planet with climate stability comparable to the Earth's around a nearby star."

'Earth's climate remains stable because the moon's gravity exerts a restraining torque on our propensity to tilt. But before the Earth's gravitational field "captured" the moon, the planet may have exhibited chaotic obliquities ranging from 0 degrees to 90 degrees, the researchers calculate.

'Because it tilts more than 54 degrees "the equator receives less radiation annually than the poles, the forecast for a moonless Earth would have been bleak", Carl Murray of the University of London writes in an accompanying editorial.

' Unhappily, Murray notes, that could be our eventual fate, because the moon is moving away from the Earth at an inch a year and one theory predicts "an obliquity near 60 degrees some 2 billion years in the future." '

But this was all written two years ago (it is summer 1995 as I write) and science, like all of us, is having to face up to a few unexpected, chaotic facts. So, here is where the fun begins.

Astronomer Mark Crealer, who cites NASA sources as saying 'something is happening out there – something that we don't understand and are absolutely powerless to stop', states that the Moon is drifting toward the Earth in a slow but inexorable fall from its orbit and, if something doesn't give, mankind will perish when worlds which have existed side by side for millions of years collide. Crealer apparently sent a memo to President Clinton warning him that 'the collision of the Moon and Earth will be preceded by devastating changes in our tides and weather in the very near future'. NASA declined to comment on the expert's report although a spokesman apparently admitted that the space agency is monitoring the position of the moon 'quite literally, around the clock'. Dr. Crealer tells us that NASA noticed a change in the Moon's position during a routine 'sky scan' on January 11th 1995. The Moon's distance from the Earth normally varies from a maximum of 254,000 miles to a minimum of 227,000 miles. But now, for the first time in recorded history, the Moon is a mere 224,000 miles away. And while that might not sound like much of a variance, astronomers agree that it is 'a potentially cataclysmic change of order in our solar system'. According to NASA, the Moon appears to be moving towards the Earth at a wildly fluctuating rate of 6 feet to 900 miles a day. And, we are told, while such erratic movement makes it impossible to predict the exact date when the Moon and Earth will collide, most experts speculate that the disaster will occur within five years. Ending on a high note, however, Dr. Crealer felt that most of us would be long dead before such an event occurs if, indeed, it ever does.

The above should not be taken too seriously at this point, however, since the full report, which I have summarized, appeared in one of the more popular American tabloids, the name of which I am reluctant to mention as I have no wish to receive angry letters from its legal representatives! However, bearing in mind my own vision of the Moon being knocked away from the Earth by some passing celestial body (see Chapter 2), and the Crop Circle message, I think that Danuih is assuring us that she herself intends to survive, as will those of all species who have elected to see in her *real* New Age.

**The Myth:**
Although Lunar divinities make their appearance in most of those early civilizations about which we have some degree of knowledge, there are certain anomalies which beg analysis. For example, did lunar worship actually begin with the Cancerian Age or did it exist in, say, Atlantean times? Colonel A. Braghine, writing in *The Shadow of Atlantis*, refers to the writings of certain classical authors affirming that several millenia before their time a large and heavily populated continent existed in the region of the Indian Ocean between Africa, Arabia and Hindustan, and probably embracing many other lands (Gondwanaland and later Mu?). Since the Moon

was not believed to have existed in such times, the writers referred
to the inhabitants as 'Preselenites'. Ancient tribal legends, old
Tibetan chronicles, Slavonic fairy tales and other ancient texts also
refer to a time when the Earth had no tidal movement and no
Moon. Here are a few more as cited by Colonel Braghine:

* The myth of the Chibchas of Columbia concerning Bohica, who
  created the Moon after a great inundation in the Funza valley.
* The myth of the Bushmen, who affirm that a large continent west
  of Africa disappeared in an epoch where there existed *two*
  moons.
* The Mayan myth concerning a great calamity during which the
  Great Serpent, i.e. a certain celestial body, was ravished from the
  heavens.
* The myth of the Tupis, that the Moon falls periodically upon the
  Earth and a new Moon takes the place of the old one in the
  heavens.
* The Aravacs of Guiana affirm that the Great Spirit sent a double
  calamity to the world: at first it was struck by fire and next a great
  flood covered the Earth prior to which, it seems, there was no
  Moon.[2]

Are we being told that two celestial displacements occurred around
the same time, the acquisition of a new satellite following the
destruction of an earlier one, or the possible involvement of
another celestial body such as a comet or asteroid? Perhaps
Hoerbiger was correct in his theory that our present Moon had a
small predecessor, the demise of which, it would seem, had a hand
in the sinking of Mu, while the acquisition of our present lunar orb
played a prominent role in the pole shift which sent Atlantis to the
bottom of the sea. For those interested in pursuing these theories
further, I have covered them in depth in my books *Atlantis: Myth or
Reality* and *Practical Atlantean Magic*.

Although the Moon is seen mostly in the feminine context this
was not always so. Lunar Gods included the Sumerian Sîn and the
Egyptian Khonsu, while Thoth (Tehuti?), the myth tells us, played
a game of draughts with the Moon which won him a seventy-second
part of her light (1/72nd of 360 is exactly 5, the five days designated
'epagomenal', from the Greek *epagomēnos* (*epi* = upon, *ageïn* = to
bring, which changed the length of our year from 360 to 365 days).

It was during those five intercalary days that the five Great Neters of the old Egyptian religion – Isis, Osiris, Horus, Set and Nephthys – appeared on the scene. Are we being told that it was at the time of or during the years preceding the acquisition of the epagomenal days, which occurred as a result of change in the orbit of Earth in relation to the Moon, that groups of people from the Old Country, anticipating the inevitable, took off to what they believed would be safer shores? The fact that the epagomenal Neters were not, according to Egyptian records, all born on the same day, which suggests that their 'arrival' was over a long period of time, rather tends to support this idea. Confirmation of this is also to be found in the Greek myth of Cronus swallowing his five children, only to vomit them up when tricked by his sixth – Zeus – who was destined to replace him (see Chapter 9). Perhaps my proposed dialogue with our lunar friend will serve to throw some light on this enigma, while also offering an explanation as to why and when the masculine/feminine or active/passive aspects became confused.

**Astrology:**
Response and fluctuation are the main astrological keywords used to describe lunar energies. The Moon, having no light of her own, reflects that of the Sun; and, in the same way, her energies, when manifest via the human condition, tend to represent the way we reflect life and all things around us. Astrologically, the Moon is all feminine, its constantly changing phases being reflected in the tides and the rhythms of feminine life of Earth. Traditionally, she rules the sign of Cancer, the mother, and her position in a natal chart is believed to tell the astrologer much concerning people's attitude towards their own mother and any progeny they may produce. Positive lunar traits include imagination, maternal instinct, receptivity, tenacity, sensitivity, while on the negative side we have faulty reasoning, inversion, unreliability and possessiveness, both of people and 'things'. The Moon in conjunction with the Sun and the Ascendant are seen as representing the three most important factors in an astrological chart.

**The Metaphysics:**
The fact that the Moon has been observed to affect adversely people suffering from mental disorders has prompted many metaphysicists to assume that its energies are more in keeping with

the psychological aspect of the human condition than the subtle. However, bearing in mind the 'field' theory and taking into account what has been discussed in earlier chapters regarding the functions of the brain, it would seem that, if the mentally afflicted are disturbed by lunar energies, the culprit is the field rather than the cerebral computer which is its lackey.

The Moon affects not only people but also animals. Having several pedigree cats I have been able to observe this first hand. I have also noted that there are 'good' Moons and 'bad' Moons. For example, a full Moon, opposing the Sun which was exactly on my fifth house Pluto, sent one of my cats missing for three weeks. The next New Moon, however, which fell on my Part of Fortune, brought him back to me. (In the horoscope of most people, the fifth house is believed to govern progeny but, since my only family is a furry one, I have noted that any afflictions thereto inevitably affect my cats.)

The effect of the Moon on the menses in women has been known for centuries, which begs the question as to what happened if, as some believe, there was a time when our planet was without a satellite. Various theories have been put forward, the most popular one being that women menstruated much less frequently, the oestrus being triggered by other planetary influences in their birth charts, or even the Sun. Many women I know have mused how nice it would be if the influence were purely solar, the inference being that they would only menstruate once a year, around the time of their birthdays! And would that not be so much better for population control? Methinks our Moon has a lot to answer for to Danuih.

Another thought which strikes me regarding my allocation of the Moon to the subtle category is that, were the fields (souls) of people (and other life forms for that matter) not programmed for a speedy return, women would not conceive as easily. All of this suggests that our satellite exerts its influence on *the field* and not simply on the brain or endocrine system.

Let us return once again to the masculine/feminine aspects of the Moon. Many Moon worshippers are horrified when I suggest that their idol also has an animus and, in my opinion, a nasty one at that. I have to confess to being totally ill at ease with lunar energies. In fact, the full Moon gives me the creeps and always has done; and yet many people I am privileged to know revel in the silver rays at their height, claiming great inspiration and spiritual benefit therefrom. The Moon's sacred metal, silver, reflects beautifully when it is clean but in time, like Dorian Gray's famous picture, it tarnishes. Although Perseus employed the polished shield given to him by Athene (Wisdom) to conquer the Gorgon (Lower Self or Id), mirrors, it seems, can produce positive or negative results, depending on many factors which are not relevant to this text.

I've always found it interesting that the Moon, No. XVIII in the Tarot deck, is always associated with trickery, deceit, disillusionment, danger and error. I'm glad I am not alone in my feelings about him/her.

From the aforegoing it must be obvious to all but the most unobservant among my readers that I am viewing the ensuing dialogue with some trepidation. Shadow-boxing with chaos is like having a conversation with someone you know might take a swipe at you at any moment. And yet you have to do it in order to learn, to establish the truth. Was it not Emerson who suggested that God offers every person the choice between Truth and Repose; – we may take which we will but we may never have both? However, with Athene's help I had better enter the affray and get it over with!

**The Dialogue:**

M:  Which aspect of your personality are you intending to present to me?

MO: Both. But please, hear me. You accuse me of being devious, misleading, of having many other less desirable traits which I know frighten you especially, owing to the fact that your field does not function on a hominid frequency. Your feline experience inclines you to despise chaos, which is why the Egyptian Sekhmet was known as 'The Enemy of Chaos'. Am I not right?

M:  Yes, indeed.

MO: And yet, your feline friends are often obliged to employ chaotic forces in their attempts to restore order. You see, my energies, be they active or passive are, due to my present position as a prisoner of Danuih, purely reflective of the chaos on her surface which has been caused mainly by the hominid species. There was a time in the long past, in my days of freedom, when Danuih, Venus and I enjoyed a fine, triadic relationship. But, since nothing is ever allowed to remain the same for very long, changes inevitably occur. Regarding your earlier reference to 'good' and 'bad' Moons, bear in mind that, as my energies are essentially reflective, they are strongly affected by those of the other members of the solar family. If, for example, the aspects between a new or full Moon are inharmonious, the chaotic effects will be felt both generally and in accordance with the individual birth chart, and likewise when the rays are harmonious.

M:   I am hearing your animus, am I not?

MO: Yes, I was the male of the trio, if you like to think in those terms, but at present I am functioning on my wrong polarity which tends to over-emphasize the chaotic aspect of my nature.

M:   So now the active/passive emphasis is all topsy-turvy, and women have been obliged to bear the brunt of this?

MO: You take it all too personally. It is but a stage in my evolvement, the cosmic development of Danuih, and therefore also of those who were drawn to be born on her surface. No-one forced them to go there. It was only because their own energies were compatible with the circumstances and experiences presented by Danuih's predicament that they now find themselves in an uncomfortable position. But, rest assured, it will not be for long. Following future changes, when I shall be bidding Danuih a fond farewell, masculine views concerning the role of women on Earth will alter radically, and with these changes will go those restricting regimes which impose so much suffering on the physical bodies of females, while also limiting the expressions of their psyches. In your language, someone is going to change the software!

M:   And about time. But tell me, why am I so uncomfortable with you?

MO: Miscreants and policemen seldom enjoy each other's company. My energies are an irritant to your field because of your cosmic origins, both as a Paschat and a Time Essence. Although you have been forced to face up to and learn to negotiate chaos as part of your Time training, your Paschat background was a strictly orderly one. My request to you is one for compassion and understanding. The virus on Danuih's body is *not* my doing. It has resulted from the ill-deeds and cruelties of the hominid species. Tempter/temptress I am and have ever been. But there has always been the choice – succumb or master. Sadly, the large majority of hominids have chosen the former path. I simply offer that choice as part of my task as an emissary of Chaos. Has it ever occurred to you that the next stage in my development may render me an emissary of Order? If you approach me with this knowledge in mind you will find that I make a better friend than enemy. But only to those who ignore the hedonistic aspect of my energies and use them wisely. As for my feminine side, from this I say to you (and to all those who read these lines) I do care deeply for all feminine creatures and, as long as the above mentioned rules are adhered to, I can be of considerable help to the feminine psyche.

M: I have been meaning to ask you, Moon, of the many gods and goddesses who have purportedly reflected your energies, is there one name by which you would prefer to be known? After all, 'Moon' sounds so impersonal.

MO: Artemis, Diana, or any of the goddesses of he hunt are inappropriate to my nature. If you must give me a 'handle', as you say, the feminine Selene or the masculine Lucifer will do nicely. But, remember, if using the latter in particular, its dark and light aspects will respond to the darkness or light in the intention or mind of the supplicant/user. And upon that note I will leave you. Fear me not, I make a better friend than foe.

M: Thank you. I will bear your advice in mind although, like all felines, I shall naturally tread with caution.

*********

# NEPTUNE

## Astronomical Data:

Neptune, the eighth planet from the Sun, has a sidereal period of revolution around the Sun of 164.8 years at a mean distance of 4.5 x $10^9$ kilometres (2.8 x $10^9$ miles), a mean radius of 24 500 kilometres (14,000 miles) and a density 17.2 times that of the Earth. Neptune has two satellites, Triton and Nereid. The former was named after an ancient Greek sea-god, son of Poseidon, who was portrayed as having the head and trunk of a man and the tail of a fish; the latter after the Nereids, any of the fifty daughters of Nereus, a sea nymph.

## The Myth:

The allocation of the oceans and waterways of the world to Poseidon (Neptune) has already been covered in Chapter 5, and it is interesting to note how this planet's watery associations have found their way down the pages of history. Medicine, for example, abounds with them, nephritis relating to any of various acute or chronic inflammations of the kidneys; nephrectomy is the surgical removal of a kidney; nephralgia, pain in the kidney, to name but a few. In geology, nephrite, a white to dark green variety of jade, is known as the 'kidney mineral' from its supposed power to cure kidney diseases. Similar derivations of the word also appear in other cultures, the Welsh 'Nerys' and the Egyptian Nephthys (Nebthet), being two examples.

## Astrology:

The main Neptunian keywords are given as nebulousness and impressionability, to which may be added artistry, idealism, psychism, sensitivity, imagination and a dreamy nature on the positive side, while negative Neptunian traits are often listed as deception, instablity, subversiveness, sentimentality, hypersensitivity and a tendency to build those earlier mentioned castles in the air (see Chapter 2). Neptune and Moon share much common ground, both being associated with mental illness, dreams, psychic energies, and the collective unconscious. Psychedelia of any kind falls under the Neptunian 'haze', while drug and alcohol abuse are also listed among its negative side-effects.

## The Metaphysics:

Neptune shares with the Moon an affinity with all things silvery and/or opaque. Neptunium, given by Sepharial as Neptune's sacred metal (see Chapter 4), is a silvery, metallic, naturally radioactive element, atomic number 93, the first of the transuranium elements, having a number of isotopes with mass numbers from 231-241. It was named after Neptune, being the next planet after Uranus. One cannot fail to marvel at how the most sceptical of scientists inevitably 'pick up' the right message without being aware of the fact that the idea originated from their intuitive right brain rather than their rational left.

Neptune is nothing if not devious, and, likewise his Egyptian counterpart or, maybe, his feminine aspect (?), Nephthys. Originally called Nebthet, meaning 'the lady of the house' as indicating a portion of the sky rather than an actual building (Nephthys being the Greek version of the name), Nephthys was the sister of Aset (Isis). One of the few ancient beliefs which survived the Theban pruning was the *Khet Khet* or 'double fire', the Fire of Solidification and the Fire of Dispersion, as represented by the bipolar Isis and Nephthys respectively. Nephthys is both the Concealer and the Revealer, while she is also accredited with the power of dreams. My own paraphysical experiences over many years have confirmed without doubt the diffusive nature of the Nephthian energies. Although in their more positive modes they can provide a powerful protection, due to the subtlety of their nature, casual dabblings of any kind should be avoided at all cost. The Nephthian animus, Neptune, functions in a similar fashion, strontium 90, which is also accredited to his influences, having disastrous effects on the physical form overall and the skeletal system in particular. (See also Chapter 14.) However, since we are dealing with two extremely nebulous energies, I would rather pass over to the planetary genius in question for his/her comments.


## The Dialogue:

M:  Genius of the planet Neptune, may I address you?

N:  But, of course. Surely you must know by now that I and my lady are your allies?

M:  Apologies. I am thinking more of any reader who might presume to be too familiar and end up lost in one of your 'mists'. So, tell me, who am I addressing, you or Nephthys?

N:  We speak as one, and we have little to say to you as you have already been employing our energies in the writing of this book. We have both watched you during your journeys through Time and will continue to so do until you take your final leave of the Mother.

M:  Have you any advice for our readers as to how you can best help them?

N:  By using our diffusive qualities. By pouring cold water onto the flames of hatred, greed, anger, and violence of any kind. A word of warning, however, which many will not like but which, nevertheless, has to be said. Access to the *genuine* higher spheres can only be obtained via the long and arduous path of spiritual evolution. It cannot be bought in a powder, or a bottle, or in any other way whatsoever. And in using the term 'spiritual' – which I know you have been trying to avoid for fear of frightening away the more rational minded among your readers – I am NOT referring to religion of any kind but rather to the finer frequencies, and the expanded bandwidth which is essential to the negotiation thereof. No, little Time Essence, I am not afraid to use that term, because when so doing I mean it in its *true* sense, minus false connotations/ emphases placed upon it by fundamentalists of any kind, be they New Age mumbo-jumboists or established religious bodies.

M:  Have you any comment to make regarding the future of Danuih?

N:  You already have all the data you need and, as things begin to 'hot up', you will be instructed accordingly. You have been familiarized with the genetic factors involved, but it will be to me and my consort, Nephthys, that the task will fall of ensuring that everyone is in the right place at the right time. And now you must break the connection. Be at peace.

M:  Thank you, both of you. I shall close down forthwith and call this the end of the chapter.

********

Endnotes:
(1)  Hawking, S. *A Brief History of Time*, p. 187.
(2)  Braghine, A. *The Shadow of Atlantis*, p. 105.

Chapter 8

## PLANETS OF ORDER PART 1

## EARTH AND PAN –
### *THE PHYSICAL/INSTINCTIVE EMPHASIS*

The principle of Order, as we have already established, does not necessarily embrace all those things in life we might be tempted to associate with ease and comfort, nor is it necessarily contributory to the sweetness and light concept which appears to delude so many New Agers. Just as Order is the child of Chaos so Chaos is the child of Order, the alternating process being a continual one essential to cosmic progress and evolution of *all* levels/frequencies. Nothing ever stands still, all must eventually change and move on. Those ancient civilizations which possessed advanced scientific and metaphysical knowledge, and were able to marry the two areas successfully, used many symbols to denote this truth, notably the sistrum, of which Plutarch wrote:

> 'The sistrum also shows that existent things must be shaken up and never have cessation from impulse, but as it were be awakened up and agitated when they fall asleep and die away. For they say they turn aside and beat off Typhon (Set) with sistra, signifying that when corruption binds nature fast and brings her to a stand, (then) generation frees her and raises her from death by means of motion.

'Now the sistrum has a curved top, and its arch contains the four (things) that are shaken. For the part of the cosmos which is subject to generation and corruption, is circumscribed by the sphere of the Moon, and all (things) in it are moved and changed by the four elements – fire and earth, water and air. And on the arch of the sistrum, at the top, they put the metal figure of a cat with a human face, and at the bottom, below the shaken things, the face sometimes of Isis and sometimes of Nephthys, symbolizing by the faces of generation and consummation (for these are the changes and motions of the elements), and by the cat the Moon, on account of the variable nature, night habits and fecundity of the beast.'[1]

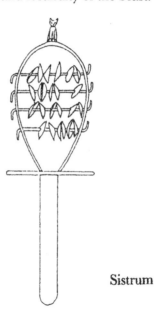

Sistrum

Plutarch (circa 46-120 A.D.), of course, based his comments on knowledge gained from the Egyptian schools of arcane learning which had sadly deteriorated by his time. But in spite of this the symbology of the sistrum, which originated in Atlantis, managed to survive. The fact that certain Egyptian priesthoods of the later dynasties had forgotten the true significance of the Primary Four may be evidenced in the fact that sistra recovered from such times often displayed only three bars, and were also minus the cymbals.

It is rather like the caduceus (see correct illustration in Chapter 6 p64), which sometimes appears in modern versions with either a singular encircling serpent or multiple encirclements from two upwards.

So, what Plutarch learned from those in the 'know', and which I am endeavouring to emphasize at this point, are the virtues *and vices* of both Order and Chaos, and that goes for the energies emitted by planets within our solar system which affect all things on Earth.

# EARTH

**Astronomical Data:**
As I have covered this aspect in considerable depth in *The Gaia Dialogues* I intend to effect a précis only. Our planet, or Danuih as she prefers to be known, was, according to science, born some 4,600 million years ago, the formation of her crust, the continents and the oceans taking place during the Pre-Cambrian era (prior to 570 million years ago). Judging her evolutionary progress against the analogy of the triple Goddess – Maiden, Mother and Crone – she appears to have approached that age, both in soma and field, where she is about to accept the role of the latter. In other words, she is due for a change, a 'retirement', if you like, from the harsh realities of life on her surface and in particular the physical injuries inflicted upon her by the chaotic nature of the hominid virus.

Astronomy defines Earth as the third planet from the Sun, having a sidereal period of revolution about the Sun of 365.26 days at a mean distance of 149.6 million kilometres (92.96 million miles), an axial rotation period of 23 hours 56.07 minutes, an average radius of 6 378 kilometres (3963 miles), and a mass of 5.974 x $10^{24}$ kilograms (13.17 x $10^{24}$ pounds).

**The Myth:**
See Chapter 6, where the Greek saga of Gaia, her earlier association with Uranus and the intervention of Cronus (Time?) supply numerous clues as to her future.

**Astrology:**
Since it is obvious that the other bodies in the solar system exert a

profound influence on both Danuih herself and all things on her surface, it seems logical to presume that she, in turn, affects her planetary neighbours. And, from comments already received from some of these, there would appear to be an excess of the chaotic at present. However, astrologers are happy to tell us how our lives are, to an extent, dictated by our birth charts and how we handle the portents shown therein, so it seems obvious to me that Danuih also has a say in these matters, and a prominent one. For example, Dr. Michael Holmes, a psychologist from Queen Margaret College in Edinburgh, suggests that the date of birth may influence the willingness (or otherwise) to embrace new ideas. In my rather limited computer terms this would suggest an ability to discard old and outdated software and replace it with a broader, more comprehensive program.

Dr. Holmes tells us that those born in the winter are more ready to accept radical theories, while those born in the summer are more inclined to oppose them. (Hey, what about Spring and Autumn, protests this very open-minded Virgo?) Dr. Holmes stumbled across the relationship by accident when studying the rapid acceptance among physicists of Einstein's theories of relativity. At the time, an alternative explanation for the same observations existed, propounded by the Dutch physicist Hendrik Lorentz. Dr. Holmes tried to identify characteristics that determined why some supported Einstein and some Lorentz. 'I wasn't looking for birth dates at all, but they emerged.'

Comparing ten eminent supporters with nine opponents, he found that all ten relativitists were born between October and April, compared with only two opponents. He later made the same comparison among biologists who either supported or opposed Darwin's theory of evolution. Eleven of twelve evolutionists were born between October and April, but only five of sixteen anti-evolutionists.

Aggregating both results in *Nature*, December to April houses 82 per cent of the proponent's birth dates, but only 24 per cent of the antagonists. May to July accounts for none of the protagonists but 60 per cent of the antagonists.

'Does this mean astrologers are right?' questions Nigel Hawkes, Science Editor of *The Times*. 'I'm not driven to astrological explanations,' Dr. Holmes told him. 'I think environmental and climatic factors may explain it.' Influences early in childhood may have different effects depending on when they are experienced. Summer and winter also offer different diets, and light-induced hormone fluctuations. 'This may not be true today,' Dr. Holmes commented. 'All the people I studied were born before electric light, central heating, and year-round availability of different foods.' My comment? The influence of Danuih is surely obvious here. I would be interested in seeing figures produced which relate to scientists born from the fifties onwards. My guess would be that, while they would obviously still fall into Dr. Holmes' two camps – protagonists and antagonists – the evidence of entropy at work in the body of Danuih would produce some startling results!

Interestingly enough, similar research undertaken some years ago by the French psychologist Michel Gauquelin also suggested that our specific talents and inclinations are blueprinted in our birth charts. So, who am I to question the experts, although one cannot fail to observe that they are frequently given to changing their minds (or orientations) in order to conform with new and perhaps more politically correct theories.

In view of the evidence it would seem that Danuih exerts her influence over us via the various seasons and other elemental phenomena while, according to heliocentric (Sun-centred) astrology in which system the Earth is always exactly opposite the natal Sun, the Sun's role in the proceedings must obviously affect not only Danuih herself, but also all the life-forms on and around her surface. Add to this the incoming influences from the Zodiac and the fixed stars and the picture becomes more complex and less localized. Complexity or reductionism – take your pick.

**The Metaphysics:**
The Danuih/Pan partnership was well known to the ancients in the form of the Earth Goddess and the Green Man, the latter being a personalized aspect of nature. It has been said that in Gaia's garden there is a cure for everything. This being the case then surely Pan, who is also a healer, is her gardener? In normal circumstances, Earth and Pan should act as earthing terminals for those orderly energies which serve us well when chaos prevails in our lives and, once her body has been healed and her axial position corrected, Danuih's orderly energies will once more unite with those of Pan to bring harmony to all surviving life-forms on her surface.

Danuih's role in the Solar School was clearly defined by her in

*The Gaia Dialogues*. Music and Healing, or Harmony and Balance, were the subjects she was given to teach. But sadly this earthly hospital/music college has become overrun by the spiritually sick who have imprisoned the doctors and nurses and are making hay with the drug cupboards, while the healing harmony of music has become fouled by sounds more appropriate to one of those 'cosmic nurseries' so beautifully described by the Crystal People (see *The Paschats and the Crystal People*). In other words, there are, on Earth at present, many fields with limited bandwidths (young souls), who should not be here in the first place, and whose presence is adding to Danuih's frustration. How can she ply her arts if she is stymied at every turn by the agents of chaos on the one hand and immature fields incapable of handling her true energies on the other? However, help is at hand in the form of her immediate family and, perhaps, a corrective body (celestial physician?) from the Oort Cloud, or some other such point in outer space.

When we suffer from a virus our bodies become heated, we run a high temperature, that being the natural way in which our immune system deals with an intruder (see Dr. John Gribbin's conversation with Professor Sir James Lovelock, in Chapter 1). Danuih, or Gaia as so many prefer to call her, has started to effect the heating program via which she will eventually eject the virus that is tearing her apart; and that virus is, according to many scientists and metaphysicists, the hominid race! But take heart for, as Plato told us so many centuries ago, there is never a major catastrophy without those left to tell the tale.

**The Dialogue:**
Having had such long conversations with Danuih in *The Gaia Dialogues*, I was reluctant to worry her in her present condition with questions she has already answered in some detail. I therefore planned to skip this one until the morning of writing this when, in the company of Bast the Cat goddess and the leonine Sekhmet, she made her presence felt and indicated her wish to renew our dialogue.

D: Thank you, elemental sister, for allowing me to speak to you as I have things that need to be said. I see you trying desperately hard to explain my plight to others but without success; and yet you have no problem understanding my situation. This is because you were born with the knowledge. Also, you were prepared fieldwise for your work here (and other cosmic tasks) in the timeless worlds of non-locality. May I therefore make a few suggestions which will, I trust, help those hominids who wish me well but fail to understand the nature of my plight, to know exactly what they are up against. When you visit a foreign country, the language, customs and culture of which are totally alien to your own, in order to facilitate communication the done thing is, I believe, to consult the guide books or, at least, glean some information concerning the ways of the people beforehand. When endeavouring to comprehend my predicament the first thing to bear in mind is that I am *not* of the hominid evolutionary strain. I am an entity from an entirely different life-stream which means that, like those foreign countries you visit, my culture, values and thinking processes bear no resemblance to your own. It would therefore be in both our interests if, before you bombard me with 'kind thoughts', you first find out something about me; the age of my body, the comparatively short time I have accommodated your species, my cosmic roots in the elemental kingdoms, my view of *all* life forms on and around my surface as conscious entities, and the fact that, although I am basically watery by nature, I am not impressed by the kind of hominid sentimentality which is not tempered by logic. In other words, I do not think like you do, nor do I conform to your psychology, so please refrain from committing the major hominid sin of seeing me in your own image and likeness and therefore expecting the kind of emotional response from me that you would expect from one another. I cannot help noticing how your scientists have gleaned a far more accurate picture of my true nature than the majority of your mystics. This is because the former have done their homework, while the latter have tended to project their own irrational and sentimentally based feelings onto me. So, while the healing thoughts and kind intentions of the enlightened few are understood and appreciated, it may take the majority of humankind some time to fully understand who and what they are dealing with. While I appreciate that this will not be possible for many, what would help me more than all the meditations and loving thoughts would be some practical application of those 'good intentions', such as ensuring the care and safety of the mineral, plant and animal kingdoms, fighting pollution and helping the environment generally.

M: Thank you, Danuih. There are several dear people I know who try so hard to help you by sending their thoughts of love and healing without being fully cognizant of who and what you actually are. As for my own, minute role, having this knowledge is a heavy burden to bear and, as you well know, I would much rather live in the comfort of ignorance. Sometimes I feel I am in prison here and circumstances -- some beastly, some benign -- are my warders. Since childhood I have viewed the world as though through the vizor of a space-suit. As a result, looking sideways on has always proved difficult, while lack of the kind of physical coordination which comes so easily to the normally functioning hominid body has caused me much distress (and cost me more than one relationship).

D: I know the frustration you experience being in an alien body; nothing seems to work as you would wish and you therefore feel intimidated and totally unable to 'hold your own'. And yet, when it comes to the crunch, your 'external' allies have always come to your aid, although they are precluded from removing the material burdens from you completely. So, take heart because we, like the hominid species, also look after our own. While on the subject of aliens, there is some important advice I would like to give. While there are some 'aliens' incarnate among you there are not as many worldwide as might be supposed. Of Paschats there are less than thirty, of Crystal People there are around one hundred, most of these within the scientific community. Others include the benign beings from the Auriga area whom I have referred to as 'the Lizard People', while the largest contingent came from another system where their planet was devastated by the ill-use of solar energies. However, the majority of the latter have been drawn to another country across the waters and, coming originally from a similar hominid strain to that of humankind, they have found adaptation easier. Of course, it could be argued that, as I said in my original dialogues, no hominids are my children as they all originated elsewhere, but some, like yourself, are comparative newcomers to the hominid experience, and it is for these that

I request patience and understanding from their fellow travellers. After all, my Earthlings, they will not be among you for very much longer, as their task will soon be completed. And, while on the subject of aliens, again I repeat my original triple warning:

1. Do not trust all that purportedly comes from 'outer space'.
2. Do not believe *all* the tales you hear about alien abductions.
3. Take no heed of what your Governments tell you concerning these matters, the two main reasons being 'concealment' and 'fear' through lack of real knowledge as to what is actually going on.

M: Two questions have arisen from our former dialogues. One concerns your rulership of Cancer which has now been usurped by the Moon; and the second, the positive/active side of your nature which you intimated would be taking control after the pole shift.

D: Although, for the purpose of my experience with the soma you call 'Earth', I have elected to place the strongest emphasis on the passive/receptive aspect of my personality, like you all I am, of course, a duality which will in the fullness of time become reconciled in the androgynous state essential for the negotiation of the regions of the Time Lords. However, I have by choice deemed it prudent to emphasize my 'active' aspect during the period immediately following my axial shift, to facilitate my personal negotiation of the new frequencies and assist all those destined to survive to do likewise. As for the rulership of the zodiacal sign of Leo, which your astrologers have at present allocated to our Mother Sun, this will all alter in time. You must understand that the Mother influences *all* signs, and only appears to connect more with Leo than with the others because she holds that guardianship pending its takeover by another celestial body during the next century in your Earth time. At present I can tell you no more as the drama has yet to unfold and there is always the chance that the actors may fluff or forget their lines. Only the Time Lords know the outcome and they are not telling. So, to your readers I have nothing more to say. But to you, sister of the fifth element, my advice is: hold tight and fear not for, when the boat starts to rock,

Neptune will be there to steer your small craft through the Symplegades.*

M: On behalf of my readers, all those concerned with your well-being and, of course, myself, thank you Danuih.

(*The Symplegades were two rocks at the entrance to the Black Sea that clashed together intermittently, but remained apart when Jason and the Argonauts passed through in the *Argo*. Mircea Eliade comments:

'The Symplegades shows us the paradoxical nature of passage into the beyond, or, more precisely, of transfer from this world to a world that is transcendent. For although originally the Other World is the world after death, it finally comes to mean any transcendent state, that is, any mode of being inaccessible to fleshly man and reserved for "spirits" or for man as a spiritual entity.'[2])

********

# PAN

**Astronomical Data:**
The existence of this extra-Plutonian planet has been affirmed by leading astronomer Patrick Moore although at present there is little data available as to its actual position or behavioural pattern other than Dr. Muses' comment on page 21 Chapter 2.

**The Myth:**
Essentially a nature deity, Pan was believed to have been the product of a union between Hermes (Mercury) and Goat Amaltheia to whom is attributed the role of wet-nurse to Zeus, Father of the Gods, for which service she was placed in the heavens as the sign of Capricorn. According to the myths, all the Olympians exploited Pan. Apollo wheedled from him the art of prophecy and Hermes copied a pipe he had left lying about, claimed it as his own invention and promptly sold it to Apollo. In spite of his divinity a story was passed around that the great god of Nature had died. It was told by

an Egyptian sailor named Thamus, who claimed to have heard a spirit voice tell him to announce, upon reaching Palodes, that the great god Pan was dead. What Thamus probably heard was the ceremonial lament 'The all-great-god Tammuz is dead', which was ritually chanted at certain times of the year.

During Plutarch's time, in the second half of the first century AD, Pan was very much alive, with shrines, altars and caves dedicated to him being regularly frequented. To the Greeks of old Pan was not so much a half-man, half-goat as an individuated nature force to which they could easily relate. He was never a vicious or sinister deity; quite the reverse, in fact, being a god of song, dance and merriment.

In the early days of Christianity, in an effort to suppress nature worship, the adherents of the Christian cult adopted the Pan figure to epitomize the concept of evil. This produced some unfortunate repercussions in the ensuing centuries when many innocent people were persecuted as devil worshippers simply because they possessed knowledge of herbs, healing and husbandry. Sadly, such ignorance still exists, many fundamentalist Christians believing paganism or Wicca to be synonymous with Satanism. However, the latter is actually a perversion of Christianity. In other words, one has to believe in the Christian concept in order to acknowledge the existence of Satan and debase Christian practices; neither of these beliefs are involved in genuine paganism or pananimism.

The new eco-awareness, however, is slowly opening the doors for Pan's return. We may refer to things 'green' in terms of Gaia, or earth-consciousness, but whatever the tag there is plenty of evidence in this day and age to suggest that this benign Greek deity is far from deceased.

Pan's association with music is highlighted in the tale of how he challenged Apollo to a musical contest, over which King Midas presided. Pan was unfortunately beaten and Apollo henceforth acknowledged as the god of Music, the seven-stringed lyre becoming his attribute. Pan, however, had his pipes, with which he continued to bring music and merriment at less exalted levels.

### Astrology:

Those astrologers who do accept the existence of Pan, and there are far more than one might expect, are inclined to accord him rulership of the zodiacal sign of Taurus, his associations with

Spring and all things growing tending to support this. Pan, like Apollo, is musical, and many musicians of note are born in the sign of Taurus, or have that sign prominent in their charts.

## The Metaphysics:

Pan's association with the instinctive aspect of the hominid nature being highly evident, I designated him as one of the three 'Tutors' in my *Olympus; An Experience in Self Discovery*, Chiron covering the Rational and Silenus the Intuitive. Some people function more strongly on the instinctive than the rational and intuitive, although the first and last tend to go together. Fields with wider bandwidths (old souls) are seldom enamoured by the bright lights of the city, tending to find more solace and pleasure in the silence and beauty of the countryside. Of course it can be argued that there is as much barbarity in country practices as anything the inner cities are likely to throw up but, on the other hand, spiritual maturity tends to bring with it an understanding of those who function predominantly at the instinctive level *because they know no better*. And it should also be borne in mind that the 'nature' which usually supplies them with their daily needs (and profits) is akin to their own instinctive natures, although there are, of course, instances where the ethics of instinctivism come in for criticism, notably in the treatment of the animal kingdom which no truly enlightened being would condone.

The idea of Pan being 'dead' could also refer to that stage in the development of humankind (and possibly many other life forms on the body of Danuih) when the instinctive is jettisoned in favour of the rational, which in turn gives way to the intuitive. Only when all three are in balance is the field ready for its cosmic extension.

Pan's growth factor is stimulative rather than creative, hence his partnership with Danuih which, for many centuries, bore excellent fruit. However, the withdrawal of either of these energies (as the myths tell us) can have dire results on both the ecology of the planet itself and those life forms that rely on it for their sustenance. In other words, we need Pan as much as Danuih does.

Since the question of Pan's passive aspect is bound to arise I searched the myths for a clue. His great love was Selene, the Moon, whom he seduced by disguising himself in the fleece of a dazzling white ewe upon whose back he spirited her to his home in the forest. On their arrival he then assumed the shape of a white ram and had his way with her. Here we are once again referred to the underlying, complex relationship between Danuih, Venus and Selene (Lucifer). It has been suggested to me by Pagan friends that Pan is actually Danuih's alter-ego or active aspect, hence the aforementioned connection between the Green Man and the Earth Goddess. Perhaps he will be able to throw some light on it for us.

## The Dialogue:

M: Pan, is there any chance that you might engage in a conversation with me?

P: I should be delighted to so do.

M: There are certain occult legends concerning your powers about which I would like to ask you. The first is the fact that you *never* appear to human beings face on, preferring to stand behind them, and, secondly, the sound of your voice, which is believed to carry magical properties.

P: No problem. The reason I *appear* to stand behind people rather than confronting them is that, were I to adopt the former pose, they would be fully exposed to their own instinctive natures which, if not tempered by the rational (they wouldn't believe it was happening in the first place), or intuitive (they were subconsciously, if not consciously aware, of my role in the cosmic scheme of things), might well blow a few fuses or, as you might prefer to say, result in a systems overload! As to my 'voice', which is the sonic of nature on this planet, few are capable of enduring such a sound having cut themselves off from all understanding of the truth concerning pananimism. They see the flowers, trees, grass, brown earth, etc. as inanimate things with no consciousness, which could not be further from the truth. Meanwhile, Nature in turn observes them with mistrust, because collectively it knows what they are feeling. How would your readers care to be in a room full of people who totally ignore their existence and who, as a consequence, trample all over them until they are bruised and bleeding, simply because they are too blind to acknowledge the presence of any other entity outside of their own 'tribe'? Well, that is how Nature feels about humankind. And that is why, when Danuih calls us, we will respond to her plea, along with our elemental brethren, to divest ourselves and our mother of the disease that is afflicting her.

M: You sound rather bitter, Pan. Surely you cannot cast all humanity in the same mold?

P: Indeed not. As you have already been told, my brother Neptune will ensure that those who carry the sleeper gene about which Danuih has told you (your fancy name for it being an allele?) and who are therefore destined to survive, will be in the right place at the right time. The rest of humanity will fall into two main categories: those whose immune systems are unable to cope with the new frequencies and who will naturally die of illness and those (mainly in your inner cities) who will end up killing each other. Order will eventually be restored and then it will be my job to ensure that all the newly exposed lands, which have been resting beneath ice or water for so many centuries, are ready and fertile for the survivors to build thereon their Golden Age.

M: What is your role in the Lucifer/Venus/Danuih complex?

P: I am not part of Danuih's psychology but a being in my own right, whose work is concerned mainly with all growing things within nature and the plant kingdoms in particular. The myth you referred to earlier simply relates to the Moon's influence on the growth factor generally. If you must accord me a passive aspect, there is always the nymph Syrinx, to whom I owe the gift of my pipes, the music derived therefrom providing me with ample opportunity for the expression of the song and dance which fully satisfies my 'anima'!

M: I am glad to hear you mention that jollier side of your personality which I have come to know and love. I also know you to be a great healer and that in Danuih's garden, which you so lovingly tend, there is a cure for everything. There will be those among my readers who will, no doubt, be somewhat taken aback by the strength of your feelings against humankind in general. After all, the myths seem to have painted you as a happy sort of character without a care in the world.

P:  I give what I receive. To those who love my domains, who revel in the natural things of the earth, who care for, and acknowledge the life force in everything, I give music, laughter, light and growth. To you I give such things because I love you as I know you love me. But to those who have little or no understanding of my kingdoms I can only return to them what they hand out to my kind: diffidence and disdain. My sonic is the sound of that which I represent, pure and simple and, like my dear Danuih, my taste in music differs profoundly from the trashy 'noise' that passes for our art among so many humans in your present day and age. Both she and I look forward to better times, when our joint roles as healers – of all things extant on her surface – and bringers of harmony, joy and the Universal Dance of Life, will once again be felt throughout the planet you call Earth. One final word for you, beloved friend. Prior to my present role here I played a similar part in the drama that was the evolution of your old, Paschat planet, and played it well. Although we had our ups and downs we resolved them amicably, each species honouring and fully acknowledging the role of the other. The final result was in accordance with Cosmic Law. And now I am here with Danuih and, together, we face yet another holocaust in the history of the terrestrial hominid species. Wish us well, dear one, as we know you will. But shed no tears for us, for we will triumph!

M:  Thank you, dear Pan. Being deeply moved I am tearful, and can say no more. Rest assured that your cosmic friends will all be behind you in full force when the time of your travail arrives.

********

Endnotes:
(1)  Mead, G. R. S. *Thrice Greatest Hermes.*, Vol. 1 p. 344.
(2)  Eliade, M. *Rites and Symbols of Initiation*, p. 65.

Chapter 9

## PLANETS OF ORDER, PART 2

### JUPITER AND SATURN –
### *THE PSYCHOLOGICAL/RATIONAL EMPHASIS*

At first glance this pair of opposites may appear as strange bedfellows, since astrologers have always associated the former with expansion and the latter with constraint. And yet both are, in their own way, emissaries of order, albeit in different applications. Let us make Jupiter our first port of call in this category, as he featured so prominently in cosmic events which took place in 1994.

### JUPITER

**Astronomical Data:**
Jupiter, the largest planet in our solar system and 1,400 times bigger than Earth, has sometimes been described as 'a "space fossil" inside a swirling shroud of multicoloured gases'.[1] By far the largest of the planets, it has a diameter through its equator of 142 800 kilometres (88,700 miles). It is twice as massive as the other eight planets put together. Jupiter earned its 'space fossil' tag because its enormous mass and gravity have retained even the lightest of the gases from which all the planets were originally formed. According to astronomers, Jupiter is thought to resemble Earth as it was before it solidified.

Because of its great distance from the Sun – at 778 300 000

kilometres (483,600,000 miles) it is five times as far as Earth is from the Sun – Jupiter takes 11.86 Earth years to make an orbit and complete its year. But its rotation on its own axis is rapid, taking less than ten hours. The speed of rotation – 44 800 kilometres (28,000 miles) an hour – has caused Jupiter to become flattened at the poles.

Jupiter is believed to have a central rocky core surrounded by layers of liquid hydrogen, which are in turn overlaid by a deep, gaseous atmosphere of liquid helium. Only the multicoloured cloud tops can be seen from Earth. These are bitterly cold, about -150 degrees C (-238 degrees F), but Jupiter is certainly hot at its core, around 30,000 c (about 54,000 degrees F). It emits more heat than it can receive from the Sun – perhaps as a result of slow contraction under its own gravity. No manned craft can approach the planet because of the intense zones of radiation surrounding it. However, the 747lb kamikaze space probe Galileo hit the atmosphere of Jupiter at 106,000 miles per hour on 7 December, 1995, and scientists are hoping that the mission will uncover new clues as to how the Sun and planets formed and how they continue to interact and evolve.

Jupiter's gaseous surface is streaked by dark belts and bright zones; the former being regions of descending gas. The colours are vivid and there is one remarkable feature, the Great Red Spot, whose colour may be due to the presence of phosphorus. Jupiter has a family of 16 satellites, four as large as planets. Its largest moons are Io, which is red and slightly larger than the Earth's Moon and has active volcanoes; Europa, which is a little smaller than Io with a smooth, icy crust; Ganymede, with a diameter of 5000 kilometres (about 3,100 miles) but larger than the planet Mercury; and Callisto, which is also larger than Earth's Moon. Both Ganymede and Callisto are icy and cratered. As for the planet's famous 'Red Spot' it is 48 000 kilometres (about 30,000 miles) across at its greatest dimension; so large that the Earth could fall into it without touching the sides.

July 16th, 1994, witnessed the commencement of the bombardment of the great planet by pieces of a comet named Shoemaker-Levy the 9th after its discoverers. There was much speculation at the time as to the effect this would have on both Jupiter itself and the rest of the solar system which, of course, includes our own planet. General scientific opinion inclined to the belief that Jupiter would undergo a radical change following the impact, although there was no shortage of sceptics who were obliged to eat their words. In *The Gaia Dialogues*, which was written prior to the event, Danuih alluded to the incident as a quantum leap for Jupiter himself, while referring the reader to the 'ripples in the pond' effect she had mentioned earlier in the book (Chapter 9, page 119) in which she stated: '... when any particle, be it as minute as a quark or as large as Jupiter, effects a quantum leap, this sends out ripples of energy in much the same way as if you drop a stone into a pond. Therefore many, many fields, be they accompanying particles (with bodies) or simply waves in non-locality, are affected by it.' She also mentioned continued changes in weather conditions worldwide, but nothing more dramatic, for the time being, anyway. In fact she has, to date (as I write, in the summer of 1995), been correct in her prognostications, a term I prefer to 'prophecies' since the latter surely implies a peep into a future the details of which might still be in the melting pot.

There has also been some speculation in metaphysical circles regarding the possibility of a 'second sun' entering our solar system, while according to other 'communicators' Jupiter himself could become a Sun. Being somewhat sceptical regarding both of these concepts I sought advice from an astronomer of note who assured me that Jupiter is far too small to initiate hydrogen fusion. Its mass would need to be about 100 times larger to do that. But, could technology ever reach the point that Jupiter could be ignited? I asked. After all, that was the premise of a sci-fi movie called '2010' (a sequel to '2001: A Space Odyssey'). My informant obviously thought not. But once again Time will tell. As to the 'second sun' idea, his comment was unrepeatable, and anyone who has studied the life-cycle of stars will know why. (See Chapter 12.)

But to return to the Jupiter bombardment: as the first colour pictures from the Hubble Space Telescope rolled in the popular press featured such headlines as 'JUPITER FIREBALL THAT WAS HOTTER THAN THE SUN'. When Fragment G from the comet struck, it exploded with the force of six million megatons of TNT, far larger than all of the world's nuclear bombs put together. It created a fireball five miles wide with a temperature of at least 14,000 F, hotter than the surface of the Sun. Instruments aboard NASA's Galileo spacecraft, which was 150 million miles away at the time, recorded the expansion of the fireball within about 90 seconds of impact to hundreds of miles across and a drop in temperature to 260 F. So, all in all, the mighty orb took something of a beating. But to what effect and, if Danuih is correct, how will this quantum leap affect us? Let us see if there are any clues to be found in the myths.

## The Myth:

The Jupiter archetype has surfaced in most of the major mythological cycles. In ancient Greece he was Zeus, father of the gods; in India, Indra; while to the Norse and Germanic peoples he was Thor, to name but a few. All these deities sported the thunderbolt as their attribute, suggesting a connection with atmospheric phenomena. According to the *Larousse Encyclopedia of Mythology*, the name 'Zeus' contains the Sanskrit root '*dyaus*' and the Latin '*dies*', which evoke the idea of the luminous sky. The Zeus/Jupiter gods were therefore seen to rule over the sky and all atmospheric phenomena: winds, clouds, rain, thunder and lightning, etc.[2]

How Zeus and his Olympians came to usurp the role of the earlier deities is a tale in itself. However, a brief synopsis is essential if we are to understand the nature of the archetypal energies with which we are dealing. Following the Uranus episode (see Chapter 6) when the old god was reduced to impotence by his son, Cronus (Time) liberated his brothers, the Titans (with the exception of the Cyclopes and the Hecatoncheires) and formed the new dynasty. Cronus married his sister, Rhea, who gave him three daughters and three sons: Hestia, Demeter and Hera; and Hades, Poseidon and Zeus. However, it seems that an oracle gave Cronus the idea that one of his sons might supplant him so he swallowed each of his children as it was born. This naturally caused Rhea much distress so, when she was about to give birth to Zeus, she sought the aid of her own parents, Uranus and Gaia, to help save the child. On their advice she went to Crete and brought forth her son in a deep cavern on the hillside. Gaia then took the newborn child while Rhea wrapped an enormous stone in swaddling clothes and presented it to the unsuspecting Cronus who swallowed it forthwith.

Meantime, Gaia had carried her grandson to the safety of Mount Ida where he was wet-nursed by Goat Amaltheia. As mentioned earlier, Zeus, in gratitude, later placed this fabulous creature among the constellations. Earth spirits helped raise the young Zeus in the forests of Ida until such times as he had grown strong enough and sufficiently wise to effect his vengeance on his father. Metis, daughter of Oceanus, gave Cronus a draught which caused him to vomit up the stone and with it Zeus' two brothers and three sisters. Thus vanquished by the might of Zeus, Cronus was driven from the sky to the very depths of the Universe. The reign of the Twelve Olympians, under their leader, Zeus, had begun.

It would seem that we are still within the boundaries of that reign when Jupiter, the mighty, exerts a truly powerful influence on us all. But what if the 1994 incident has in some way reduced that influence, thus changing the status quo? Are the astronomical facts regarding the bombardment of the Great Planet indicative of a change of emphasis throughout this solar system? After all, Uranus was supplanted by Cronus who, in turn, was banished by Zeus. Perhaps it is time for Zeus himself to stand down, but in favour of whom? Dare we hope that he will throw some light on this and other enigmas later in this chapter?

**Astrology:**
Jupiterian traits, the text-books of astrology tell us, in addition to expansion and preservation, are especially those of the zodiacal sign of Sagittarius: outgoing, adventurous, intelligent and sporty. Positive keywords include joviality, generosity, optimism, a broad outlook, and good fortune, while negative traits include improvidence, lack of sense of detail, provocation, wastefulness, trusting too much to luck, jocosity and extremist views.

Always associated with 'good luck', Jupiter has been named 'The Greater Fortune', probably because of the expansive nature of his energies. It should also be taken into account that there is an over-expansive point at which the benign orderliness of Jupiter gives way to the chaotic, implosive energies of Pluto (see rays and anti-rays, Chapter 4). Evidence of this may be seen in those people who win large sums of money or inherit vast fortunes which they are mentally incapable of handling, the inevitable result being psychological fragmentation and eventual downfall.

Personally, I have never found Jupiter to be particularly helpful to me. I agree with astrologers regarding the general premise that he can bring extra material help, either financially or in other practical ways. But this supposed 'bonus' is usually accompanied by upheavals which inevitably absorb the 'goodies' to the extent that in the final analysis one finds oneself in an 'as you were' situation, having also experienced considerable inconvenience to boot. Whether the resultant changes prove beneficial in the long run, however, only time will tell.

## The Metaphysics:

Taking into account the information supplied by Danuih, it would seem that Jupiter's dilitatory influences have been tempered in some way. Has he now learned self-discipline and moderation? Will his new 'phase' coincide with an emphasis on the passive side of his personality, Hera, Mother of the Gods, perhaps? Over-expansion inevitably leads to 'systems-overload' at any or all levels. In the human system, for example it can lead to obesity resulting from over-indulgence in the good things of life and, as we all know, excessive material self-gratification requires plenty of spare cash. Jupiter can also be 'mind-blowing'; remember, his stimulant energy is lunar! At the subtle level the overemphasis of his energies may be observed in both the overblown egos of the many 'gurus' whose predilection for material possessions is something of a joke, and those 'holier-than-thou' spiritual snobs who revel in the growing number of their followers from whom they delight in drawing as much power (and money) as possible. Think about it!

Purveyor of Law and Order Jupiter may well be, but could he, perhaps, represent that accelerated point in order at which it automatically reverts to chaos? A thought worth considering and, if our portly friend feels up to it, perhaps he will honour us with either confirmation or denial thereof.

## The Dialogue:

M: Genius of Jupiter, I know you have suffered great pain and injuries and I am therefore reluctant to seek your advice in relation to the work in which I am at present engaged. I will not, therefore, take offence if your answer is in negative.

J: My answer is affirmative, although I have little to say at present since my own role in the future is in what you would describe as 'the melting pot'. In other words, it is as yet undefined.

M: Is this lack of definition on your part or that of the Sun or some other, more exalted, celestial genius?

J:    Some of each. You see, I have, As Danuih has told you,
      experienced a major quantum leap which has affected me both
      somatically and fieldwise. As a result, I am in the process or
      reorganizing my energies to see how they can be best used in the
      future rearrangement of the solar system.

M:    May I take it from this that there will be physical adjustments
      in the planetary bodies in our solar system as a result of
      Danuih's pole shift?

J:    Danuih's change of axis will affect us all. Of course there will
      be rearrangements but, rest assured, I will NOT suddenly turn
      into a sun nor, as your astronomers will be happy to inform
      you, is such a body likely to conveniently float into this system,
      such behaviour being inconsistent with the nature of stars.

M:    Your influences, as far as astrology is concerned, have always
      been viewed as expansive and fortunate. Will this now cease to
      be so?

J:    You know the answer to this full well but, for the benefit of your
      readers, I will confirm that the energies I will be emitting *once
      my wounds are healed* will differ from those formerly associated
      with me. You are correct in your assumption that I represent
      the point in the solar system at which order turns to chaos, while
      (and here is a piece of information which is relevant to an earlier
      chapter) Uranus plays a similar role in the conversion of chaos
      to order. More of my own role in the future I am not at liberty
      to divulge for the moment.

M:    May I ask why, as The Greater Fortune, do you appear to bring
      good luck to some but difficult times to others?

J:    The principle of expansion is designed to work at the level best
      suited to the individual. Winners of State lotteries and other
      such unearned gains tend to contact that aspect of my energies
      which automatically reverts to chaos, hence the tragedies
      which frequently afflict many of the lives of such people. On the
      other hand, expansive energies which home into broader fields
      (old souls), or subtle, more exalted levels of consciousness, can

effect changes which may appear painful initially, but which are, in the long run, best for the growth experience of those concerned. Perhaps you can now see the similarities between myself and Uranus?

M: Thank you for helping me to understand. I can also see why Zeus, as the giver of Law and Order will, in the next stage of the cosmic drama, give way to a new planetary genius in the same way that Cronus supplanted his father Uranus and Zeus, in turn, supplanted Cronus. I know you are not prepared to tell me any more but I think I know, anyway.

J: Then you would be advised to keep such information to yourself, for the time being. Let people work it out for themselves. Your astronomers, of course, will get there ahead of your mystics, but that is simply because, as you have already been told, some very advanced beings whose roots were in another part of the galaxy (and another universe, prior to that) have taken bodies within your scientific community.

M: I sense that you wish to stop at this point?

J: You sense correctly. I wish for peace but, if there are those among you who have my welfare at heart and are so gifted, then healing energies would be far more appreciated than efforts to contact me as I would rather be left alone, for the time being.

M: Then I thank you, and apologize for taking up your time. After all, time is energy. And I wish you well in the now, and much success with your future role.

********

# SATURN

**Astronomical Data:**
Saturn, one of the outer planets of the solar system, is second in size only to Jupiter and visible to the naked eye as a bright, yellowish

star. Saturn's overall density is less than that of water, and it probably has a rocky core surrounded by layers of liquid hydrogen, which are in turn overlaid by a gaseous atmosphere, the actual surface we can see. The cloud tops are very cold, at a temperature of about -180 degrees C (-292 degrees F). But the core must be hot since Saturn radiates more energy than it receives from the Sun.

The main glory of Saturn is its magnificent system of rings, visible with a small telescope, which are composed of icy particles (seen clearly by Voyager space probes). There are two main rings, separated by a gap known as Cassini's Division, and various less conspicuous rings. The Voyager space probes have shown that the rings are very complex, being made up of thousands of individual thin rings separated by gaps.

Saturn has a wealth of satellites; nine were known before the flights of the Pioneer and Voyager space probes, and today at least 20 are known. Most of them are comparatively small, but there is one large satellite, Titan, which is 5800 kilometres (3,600 miles) in diameter, bigger than the planet Mercury. Titan has a dense atmosphere composed chiefly of nitrogen, with considerable quantities of methane. On Titan's surface, hidden by a reddish photochemical smog, there may be cliffs of solid methane, rivers of liquid methane, and a methane drizzle from the clouds. Three of Saturn's moons – Tethys, Dione and Rhea – show as bright spots below Saturn, and Tethys casts its shadow on the planet. Computer-enhanced colour pictures of Saturn's rings record differences that may be caused by chemical variations from one part to another. The lumps of icy material which make up the rings range from the size of a house to that of coins. The outermost ring contains two strands twisted round each other and this braided effect is believed to be caused by Saturn's magnetic field.

**The Myth:**
Saturn is, of course, Cronus, he who castrated his father and was in turn supplanted by Zeus (Jupiter) which surely tells us something about the changing roles of the planetary genii in our solar system. Since the mythological details of these nefarious activities are given in Chapter 6 there is no need for repetition. However, the staggering accuracy of the information which has come down to us via the myths never ceases to amaze me, especially in the light of Jupiter's prognostications regarding changes of *status quo* in our

solar system in the future.

## Astrology:

Although 'limitation' and 'cold' are astrology's two main keywords for Saturnian energies, he is also believed to endow those born under his specific influence with caution, control, patience, responsibility, seriousness and thrift or, alternatively, the negative traits of depression, dogmatism, fear, limitation, severity, lack of inspiration, dullness and a grasping nature. However, as has already been discussed, how one reacts to Saturn's energies is a personal matter, although he does tend to add a certain 'weight' to whatever he touches, which is probably one of the reasons why the ancients allotted him lead as his special metal.

## The Metaphysics:

Saturn's association with Time and science is interesting. Observe how, according to certain authorities (see Chapter 8) his position both by zodiacal and planetary placings inclines people towards the sciences and other analytical studies. As I understand it, in the school that is our solar system Saturn is the Headmaster or Supreme Tutor. It is he who marks our exam papers and decides whether we are ready to pass through Pluto's gates to the freedom of the galaxy beyond. Although both Saturnian and Jupiterian influences tend to work mainly at the psychological/rational level, Jupiter's lessons appear at first glance to be simple when compared to the severity of Saturn's examination requirements. What may appear to be easy situations, however, can often turn out to be dangerous and difficult to handle, while those tasks we approach with trepidation can, providing we have done our homework, prove to be the most rewarding in the long run. I have heard it said that 'Saturn hooks you but Jupiter lets you off the hook'. True, but once free of Saturn's safety strap one is left to sink or swim in the vastness of Jupiterian abundance; and, as evidence has shown only too well, there are many who simply cannot handle 'too much too soon'. Personally, I am happier with Saturn, but then, as the Moon and others have pointed out, I am a 'law and order person'. Square? Do me a favour, I am positively *cubic*!

Certain planets in our solar system may be observed to enjoy a close relationship with the Time Lords. Mercury represents the chaotic approach to Time and Saturn the orderly. The fact that both of these planets appear under the psychological/rational categories must surely tell us something. My own interpretation of this would be that we need to rationalize both the instinctive and intuitive in order to create a format suitable to life on this planet. Too much of the former excludes us from learning the whys and wherefores of our life on Earth, while too much of the latter inclines us to the kind of irrational mysticism which creates the barrier between physics and metaphysics.

Saturn, as I see it, tends to slow time down, hence his association with old age. Mercury, on the other hand, with his accent on youth, speeds it up. Saturn is the punitive Master who does not spare us (or rather, allow us to spare ourselves!). None of the currently favoured 'politically correct' stuff for him; were he to voice his views he would probably, with true north country bluntness, 'call a spade a ruddy great shovel'! Perhaps I am doing him an injustice here, so why not ask him to speak for himself?

## The Dialogue:

S:  I intend to get in first on this one and, since you and I are old friends, I know you will not be offended by my effrontery.

M:  On the contrary, I love it. Please continue.

S:  My piece will be brief for I am not given to loquacity. Besides, Neptune has already broached the subject so here it is for what it is worth. There is no easy way to wisdom, and by 'wisdom' I mean field bandwidth or, to use your term, 'soul-age'. You cannot buy it, you cannot learn it in a few weekend sessions, nor can you hope to achieve it by rubbing shoulders with someone who has moved a little further along the Path than yourself, the latter situation often leading to much ill-will from the student and pain to the teacher. As has already been said, Hercules had Twelve Labours and so has everyone else on this planet unless, of course, they passed the equivalent elsewhere in the Cosmos and are simply back here at present in some 'ministerial' capacity! How I dislike the appendage 'Master', and hasten to agree with Danuih's summing up of the situation in that most of the so-termed 'Masters' preached about by your mystics and

and esotericists are purely figments of the hominid imagination: pictures conjured up by electrical impulses in the brain which are struggling to express the infinite in finite terms – and their particular version of it to boot – against which they aspire to measure their own 'spiritual' progress.

The hominid students in the school of which I am Head Teacher appear to be obsessed with personalizing celestial energies, a practice which inevitably leads them into trouble as they so often end up putting the wrong name to the wrong character. A classic example of this is in your Scriptural story of the battle between darkness and light (order and chaos) as epitomized by Lucifer and Mikaal (or St. Michael as some prefer to call him). The latter dispels the former, you are told, as though all this happened in the past when, in fact, the reference, were it correctly interpreted would tell you about the future. Let us take the story from another, more futuristic angle; Lucifer (the name by which the Moon has indicated that he wishes to be known) will be removed from his existing orbit around the Earth by a member of a select group of beings entrusted with keeping balance (Law and Order to you) in this Universe with, of course, a little help from a passing cosmic 'physician' from the Oort Cloud. As Danuih has already told you (see *The Gaia Dialogues*), the said Mikaal is NOT a planetary genius, never has been nor ever will be. He is, if you like, a policeman or, if you prefer me to use one of your fancy metaphysical terms from the Christian tradition, a member of that devic evolutionary stream designated 'Seraphim'. Sorry to disillusion you, but there it is: take it or leave it.

M: Saturn, I am SO pleased you have voiced the above.

S: Don't be so emotional about it. That is the way things are and, as far as I am concerned, if people do not like it then they can do the other thing. They will all have to come to terms with my rules eventually in order to pass safely through the Gates of Hades, which implies a tempering of the ego with self-discipline. On the other hand, for those willing to forget their own pet theories and really *learn* I can be the kindest and most considerate of tutors (a small hint of the passive/receptive side of my nature!). The choice is there for all. And thereupon I rest my case and bid you, little feline Time Essence, a fond (sincere but untainted by false emotion!) adieu.

M: Thanks ever so. As you know, I feel very close to you so may I reiterate your final sentence and sign off with love (of the universal kind, of course!).

********

Endnotes:
(1) *Readers Digest Great Illustrated Dictionary*, Vol. 1, p. 914.
(2) *Larousse Encyclopaedia of Mythology*, p. 103.

Chapter 10

## PLANETS OF ORDER, PART 3

### VULCAN AND VENUS –
### *THE SUBTLE/INTUITIVE EMPHASIS*

While Vulcan is a comparatively unknown quantity, Venus is well represented, both scientifically and astrologically, and one of the questions put to me when discussing the contents of this book has been why I have placed the latter under this Chapter heading, since her energies are so often associated with the more material aspects of life such as carnal love and money. I trust that the ensuing pages will well and truly answer this question and, perhaps, serve to show Venus in a more subtle and spiritually refined light. However, let us first attend to our mysterious friend, Vulcan, whose very existence is highly questionable.

### VULCAN

**Astronomical Data:**

Vulcan, the eminent mathematician and scientist Dr. Charles Musès states, was named by Neptune's discoverer, the great astronomer Leverrier. Musès describes Vulcan as a single infra-Mercurial planet in our solar system, which was later denied by astronomers but which is shown to lie at a mean distance of 0.24 astronomical units (one such unit being the mean distance of Earth from the Sun) and to have a period of 43 days. He tells us:

'There is only one Bessel function zero closer than the first zero of the first order, and that is the first zero of the zeroth order, corresponding to the infra-Mercurial planet Vulcan. It would be difficult to observe since it is so close to the Sun, but one would simply have to continue suitably accurate observations throughout a period of some 45 days in order to confirm it. This has not yet been done, although a French team near Grasse had been willing to try it when work on the European satellite Hipparchus interrupted those plans in 1982'.[1]

Musès would appear to be one of the few scientists today to combine metaphysical studies with his own discipline and, speaking of archetypal access via planetary bodies (a subject I touched on earlier in this book), he has this to say concerning the energies of Vulcan:

'It is this space-independent timing of the sessions that makes possible the access of the archetypal powers associated even with bodies known by indirect means to exist, though not yet observationally positioned in space. We refer here specifically to the perturbationally indicated extra-Plutonian planet (herein called Pan as in the first serious investigation from data gathered by various observers since the 1930's and before) and the infra-Mercurial body (here called Vulcan after the name suggested by U. J. Leverrier who first suspected it). Vulcan's period of 43 days and its semi-major axis of about 0.2405 astronomical units stem from C. Musès' investigation of the basis of a viable, accurate theory for the Bode-Titius Law by means of the zeros of cylindrical wave functions of Zeroth and the first order, published by the National Research Council of Italy in 1965 (*La Ricerca Scientifica*, series 2, part 1, vol. 5, no. 10-12, pp. 200-201)[2] *Ibid*, p. 111.'

I have to confess that the mathematics here lose me but I am sufficiently confident in the worthy Doctor's scholarship to take his word for it. It seems logical to me, however, that any planet that near the Sun (if it is indeed a planet as such) must have special properties of both a physical and metaphysical nature which were well known to the originators of the myths.

Further to the above, the Astrological Association Journal, No.

XIII 4.14. featured the following Vulcanian snippet:

> 'Professor Henry Courteen claims to have discovered a
> new planet between Mercury and the Sun (see *The Observer*
> 29/6/71). Evidence collected during the eclipse of March
> 1970, indicates the presence of either a cluster of cometary
> fragments or a true planet, about 500 miles in diameter, about
> nine million miles from the Sun. Confirmation will not be
> possible until the eclipse in the summer of 1972. With a
> geocentric separation from the Sun of no more than a few
> degrees, astrologically there would be a constant conjunction
> between the two bodies.'

However, since little, of anything, has been heard of Professor
Courteen's 'discovery', we may assume that it is still considered
unsubstantiated by the astronomical fraternity as a whole, although,
as the saying goes, 'there is no such thing as coincidence!' So, to our
next port of call for further knowledge and guidance.

**The Myth:**
The smithy archetype obviously carries powerful energies since
smithy gods appear in most of the early cultures. Agni was the Vedic
god of fire, Britain had its Wayland, Egypt its Ptah; and so forth.
But probably the best documented is the Greek Hephaestus, whose
story serves us well for the purpose of this narrative. There is a
gnomey quality about Hephaestus which brings him in line with
those archetypal manifestations which are highly gifted in spite of
their rather unprepossessing appearance.

According to Homer, Hephaestus was actually born lame,
although other sources insist that, as the son of Zeus and Hera, he
was so ugly at birth that his mother threw him from Olympus.
Fortunately, he landed in the sea where he was rescued by Thetis
and Eurynome who cared for him until he was strong enough to
make a life for himself. He rewarded them with beautiful jewellery
which he made with his own hands. When news of his skills reached
his mother she made haste to fetch him back to Olympus where she
set him up in a finely equipped smithy and gave him the beautiful
Aphrodite (Venus) for a wife.

Evidence for the physical problems associated with smith
gods has been recently brought to light by archaeologists.

Apparently, the Bronze Age smelters as far back as 3,500 knew that arsenic added to metal alloys made them much more durable and they maintained the optimum content of 2.5 per cent with great accuracy. The use of this metal was later phased out, on account of its side-effects (fragility and breaking of the bones of the legs and feet), which constituted health hazards for those who made it. As it has ever been the custom for mankind to model his gods and archetypal figures on himself, smithy gods were inevitably shown with physical deformities, usually of the legs or spine, which would have been consistent with the afflictions suffered by those earthly practitioners of the smithy arts.

All the gods and goddesses had recourse to Hephaestus' skills although, in addition to such works of art as Zeus' golden throne and Demeter's sickle, he also constructed a set of golden mechanical female androids, as well as some three-legged robot tables to help him in the more menial tasks of his smithy. The indication here is, of course, that Vulcan energies are by no means limited to the ornamental. Engineering of all kinds, and building, for that matter (as with the Egyptian Ptah, Patron of Masons), come under his aegis.

Hephaestus is probably best known for his famous Net. Suspecting his wife of infidelity, he forged a net so fine that it could not be seen, but so strong that it could not be broken. One evening, as Aphrodite shared her couch with Ares, Hephaestus stole up on the couple and waited for them to fall asleep, whereupon he spread the net over them and invited the whole company of Olympus to witness how he had been betrayed, which, it seems, proved something of an embarrassment all round. Zeus finally persuaded him to let them go after extracting a promise from Ares to pay the price for his adultery.

The Ptah archetype of Egypt, however, was rather a different character, being much loved by the ordinary people, who used to invoke him when undertaking menial tasks concerned with either things mechanical or the ingenuity required in the process of construction. His consort was the lioness-headed Sekhmet, known as 'the enemy of Chaos', and their son, the gentle healer Nefer-Tem, later associated with the Greek Asclepius.

**Astrology:**
Although there are several astrologers who acknowledge the

existence of Vulcan, notably the late John Naylor, who enlightened me regarding the astrological nature of his planetary energies, little has been written about him outside of the academic circles of astrology. Naylor saw Vulcan as the rightful ruler of Virgo, according him many of the qualities normally associated with that sign, minus those normally attributed to the Mercurial influence.

## The Metaphysics:

Here is where the subject becomes interesting. Vulcan's close proximity to the Sun obviously gave rise to the myth of his fires. Therefore, those sages from the long-distant past whose scientific knowledge, I believe, gave birth to the myths, must have been well aware of the planet's existence and the role it plays in human affairs. As with the classical myths, many of the old fairy tales appear to contain encoded scientific knowledge relevant to both the past and future of our planet and the solar system as a whole. According to some metaphysicists, Vulcan represents the hidden or higher aspect of the Self: the secret builder, hidden away in his solar smithy, empowered by his mother (the Sun?). Prometheus used Hephaestus' fire to light the torch with which he gave the gift of fire (creativity) to mankind. Bronze, sacred to all the smithy gods, contains various alloys of copper and tin, sometimes with traces of other elements such as phosphorus and antimony, which serves to highlight his association with both Jupiter and Venus. He is, as it were, the 'orderly melting pot', his surface contrasting dramatically with the frozen wastes of Pluto.

Coincidentally, Hercules' eleventh Labour involved fetching fruit from the golden apple tree that had been the wedding gift to Hera from Earth herself. The 'tree' symbology features strongly here (as it does in many other mythologies), while apples have always been sacred to Venus. Interestingly enough, it was during this Labour that Hercules (humankind?) freed the tortured Titan, Prometheus, from his purgatory imposed by Zeus for releasing the divine fire to humanity, thus making the old Titan's services once more available to the species he tried so hard to help.

Is Vulcan our Prometheus, he who, according to the ancient Greeks, was the progenitor of mankind, and who played a role in the last pole shift by warning his son, Ducalion, of the impending danger? It was on the advice of his father that Ducalion constructed an ark in which to take refuge when the waters rose, a myth which was so powerful it even found its way into the scriptures of the more structured religions of today! Then there is Vulcan's passive side to consider. According to the myth Hephaestus' real love was Athene, having been instrumental in her birth from the head of Zeus; however, Athene, wishing to remain a virgin, rejected his advances. A hint, perhaps at the possibility of the passive aspect of his nature being confined to the more exalted realms of spiritual love?

Maybe it is my imagination, but I have a strange feeling regarding the role to be played by Vulcan in the cosmic drama which is due to unfold in our solar system during the next few decades. Will he be forthcoming if I ask him?

## The Dialogue:

V: But of course. After all, I have frequently conversed with you, and helped you with the occasional task, as befits my energies, under the name of Ptah.

M: How very true. It is just that I am unused to dealing with the Masonic energies via a celestial body, and especially one the very existence of which is still highly questionable.

V: You are right to be cautious. But rest assured that both my existence and the true nature of my soma will be well and truly established in the future. However, if you are still having doubts I am happy to respect your feelings so let us resume this dialogue with myself playing the role of the Ptah you know, the consort of the Egyptian Sekhmet.

M: Thank you for your understanding. I am happy to comply with your suggestion. May I ask you about your Masonic connections?

V: My Masonic connections are archetypal. In other words, as a planet, my energies reflect those of the Divine Masonic Archetype which works in concert with the Timeless Ones to effect the structural foundations of universes. As you have already explained to your students the word 'Masonic' is in itself explanatory in that it can be broken down into Ma and Sonic. In other words, sound plays a part in the fusion of particles which form the basis of matter. Words do not come into existence by accident, although I doubt whether any of those practising Masonry today would have the slightest idea as to where the Masonic concept originally arose. I hear Egypt cited as its country of origin but, in fact, the study and knowledge of sonics predated that civilization by thousands of years. When the time is right, as it will be in the future, this knowledge will once again be released into the solar system via my energies. Those who were skilled at its manipulation in days long past will be ready to return in new bodies in order to reintroduce this science to a world which will once again be capable of handling it with care, caution and benevolence. And did you not once hold a conversation with such a gentleman?

M: You mean the Nobel Prize Winner I wrote about in my book *Time: The Ultimate Energy*?

V: Correct. He will be one of the advanced guard of new scientists whose approach to their discipline will be based on different principles. Instead of learning via a series of blind trials and errors, the torture of other creatures, and all the other paraphernalia associated with modern scientific research, they will simply access the cosmic data banks and, with my assistance, effect a direct line to the archetype itself.

M: Tell me, are you really the 'ruler' of the zodiacal sign of Virgo as some astrologers have suggested?

V: I will be once certain events have taken place and I am officially 'discovered', in much the same way that Uranus has now taken the Aquarian reins from Saturn and Neptune has relieved Jupiter of his Piscean emphasis. But, for the time being, Mercury, with the help of the friendly planetoid Chiron, holds the Virgoan fort.

M: Maybe I am off key but I seem to have a sneaking feeling that your influences are somehow connected with the beliefs of certain Eastern religions. Am I right or wrong?

V: You are referring to Buddhism, of course. Well, yes and no. I have tried to introduce the concept of meditative practices into the human psyche in the hope that it would help humankind to understand that all things, animate and inanimate, have a consciousness. This has manifested to some extent in the Buddhist respect for other life-forms but failed miserably through the inevitable intrusion of the human ego. Humankind is truly sick in its erroneous concept of its own supremacy, while even most of its so-termed 'spiritual' religions are still fouled by the mistaken idea that experience in a female body is somehow inferior to that of a male. Believe me, in the final analysis there is NO difference. It is simply that the field or soul needs to experience both the masculine and feminine, *and* fully understand and come to terms with them both, before it can unite the two within itself; this uniting eventually leading to the androgynous state which is absolutely essential to its ascendance to the finer frequencies. Advanced races such as those you refer to as the Crystal People did not display marked differences between the masculine and feminine. Likewise, fields with extended bandwidths or 'old souls' (as some humans prefer to call them) who have balanced the anima and animus within themselves to the extent that they are able to understand and deal with both aspects *with comfort*.

M: I notice that you refer to the Time Lords as 'The Timeless Ones'; I like that!

V: Do you not consider it a more suitable appellation than the one you have been using? After all, they are androgynous, which means, in your terms of reference, that they are both 'Lords' *and* 'Ladies'.

M: Well, Vulcan, or should I say Ptah? I had no idea that our conversation would take this turn. I was not quite sure what to expect but I should have guessed that, as you represent the spiritual or subtle aspect of the Order Principle, you would have something to say regarding balance at that level. Tell me, were you known to the Atlanteans?

V: There is no need for me to answer that. Search your own data banks and you will find that I appeared in the form of one of the two Divine Ancestors whom you have chosen in your writings to refer to as Ta-Khu.

M: 'But surely Ta-Khu was associated with Time, in the same way as the Egyptian Thoth/Tehuti?

V: As you are well aware, just as Pluto is the Timeway-Out or exit door for those of humankind who have concluded their Twelve Labours satisfactorily, I am the Timeway-In for those who, as invited guests of the Mother Sun, have come to fulfil a specific mission. This task may be concerned simply with the observation of events, as in your own case, the somatic evolution of a certain species, or some form of transpersonal upliftment. Sadly, the latter, if effective for a short time, seldom lasts long. Manipulative forces (via the agency of humankind, other species extant on Earth having no interest in this 'power game') inevitably get hold of it and use it for their own selfish ends, the main one being to gain power over their followers. I think I have said enough. You must now turn your attentions to Venus who is 'waiting patiently in the wings' as your theatrical people are wont to say. So, although I bid you a temporary farewell, as you know I am always there when needed.

M: Thank you so much, Vulcan. You have brought back many memories which I now see more clearly.

********

# VENUS

**Astronomical Data:**

Venus, our nearest neighbour in the sky, is almost a twin to Earth in size and mass and, as it is closer to Earth than any other planet, it shines brightly in the night sky. Astronomers acknowledge her as the second planet from the Sun, having an average radius of 6 100 kilometres (3,800 miles), a mass of 0.815 times that of the Earth, and a sidereal period of revolution about the Sun of 224.7 days at a mean distance of approximately 108 million kilometres (67.2 million miles).

Startling facts concerning Venus have recently come to light via the agency of the Magellan space probe, which has revealed the face of Venus in stunning detail for the first time by computer-generated pictures sent back across 25 million miles. Gigantic craters, canyons stretching more than 4,000 miles across, peaks that dwarf Everest; a world torn and buckled by unimaginable forces. Such is the picture of Venus which challenges our scientists for explanations. Sadly these pictures will be the last Magellan will transmit. With its solar panels and gyroscopes failing after its epic five-year journey, much of it spent orbiting Venus, by the time this book is in print its life-span will be ended. However, it will continue to send its useful data back to Earth right up to the moment when the Venusian flames consume it.

During its journey of discovery, the spacecraft used radar and computers to penetrate the dense clouds of carbon dioxide and sulphuric acid that shroud the planet. Previous attempts provided only tantalizing glimpses of Venus which, at some point in its evolution, suffered a grim greenhouse effect that left it with a surface temperature of 400 degrees centigrade.

Magellan was launched in 1989 and spent 15 months on its lonely journey through space. Once in orbit it started steadily mapping the surface of Venus and radioing back data on its discoveries. Delighted NASA scientists say it has gleaned more information than previous planetary missions combined. In an article in *The Daily Mail*, Saturday, October 4, 1994, NASA expert Stephen Saunders is quoted as saying: 'Venus is truly a geologist's paradise. Our biggest surprise is that the surface is relatively fresh. We estimate that 80 per cent of the surface is covered by lava flows.' Another researcher, Moustafa Chahine, said: 'Magellan has been successful beyond our expectations. The images sent back give us unprecedented information.'

From these transmissions scientists assembled a mosaic of photographs with 10,000-mile-long 'footprint' strips of data. The planet's atmosphere is 90 times heavier than that of Earth and accumulated volcanic gases are believed to have caused the runaway greenhouse effect. On Venus all water has long ago evaporated. But the amounts of heavy hydrogen left in the atmosphere suggest there was once enough water to cover the planet's surface with an ocean 30 feet deep. 'Venus has simply boiled dry, like a kettle left too long on the stove,' say Kenneth Lang and Charles Whitney, authors of *Wanderers in Space*, a recent survey of the solar system.

Could we be getting an apocalyptic glimpse of Earth's eventual fate? Some theorists suggest our planet will also become a molten crucible of unbreathable gases. Both Earth and Venus have temperatures controlled by the Greenhouse Effect, with carbon dioxide in the atmosphere affecting the amount of sunlight. All of this may add stark significance to air pollution research carried out by the Endeavour shuttle mission, which discovered that carbon monoxide has increased above South America, southern Africa and the southern Atlantic. There was also more pollution north of Australia. The burning of grasslands and forests has been blamed for the rise; and all this has been caused by humankind. Is it any wonder that Danuih views us as a virus on her surface?

**The Myth:**

Venus, the Roman goddess of Love and Beauty, after whom the planet was named, was identified with the Greek Aphrodite. However, bearing in mind the above, one wonders how a planet with such a seemingly inharmonious body could have become associated with all that is beautiful on Earth? Perhaps a quick glance at the myth might help us here.

The Greek Aphrodite was depicted as a beautiful, seductive love goddess whose attribute, the Girdle, was so powerful that it could deflect even the thunderbolts of Zeus himself! So, where and how did this myth originate? Although Homer describes Aphrodite as the daughter of Zeus and Dione, the more popular view was that she was conceived in the foam of the ocean from the seed of Uranus, dropped there when he was castrated, her name meaning 'foam-born'. Even the Greeks admitted that she was not exclusively theirs as she was also worshipped elsewhere under such names as Astarte, Ashtaroth and Ishtar. Each pantheon appears to have its representation of the Love principle which, it is generally believed, was so strongly acknowledged by the people of ancient Greece that a character had to be built up around it.

Are we being told something about the *soul-age or bandwidth* of Venus rather than the age of her body as compared with those of the other planets in the solar system? After all, Uranus predated both Cronus and Zeus so Aphrodite, as his daughter, would have been from his devic group-soul. I cannot help feeling that there is so much we do not know and, until such information is made available to us our theories will be shrouded in the mists of doubt and uncertainty. It is also worth noting that not all pantheons represented the Love Principle in feminine form. For the Irish Celts, for example, their Love god was Angus Õg (Angus the Young), patron of all who were struck by Cupid's arrows, and restorer of life to those who relinquished their last breath in the cause of love. Associated with youth, music, beauty and charm, this deity embodied the qualities of both Aphrodite and Adonis combined, which tells us a lot about the psychology of the Celts in relation to their anima/animus balance.

## Astrology:

Astrologers call Venus 'The Lesser Fortune', indicating that, although her harmonious energies are conducive to good fortune, in these stakes she stands second to Jupiter. Harmony, unison and relatedness are her main astrological keywords, and her position in a birth chart is said to indicate the native's ability to attract others and engage in close relationships therewith. This aspect is not, however, limited to personal amours and emotional commitments but also includes business arrangements and partnerships of all kinds. Other positive Venusian characteristics include adaptability, artistry, companionship, grace, harmony, tact and a loving and peace-loving nature, while the flip-side suggests laziness, indecisiveness, unreliability, weakness and a 'peace-at-any-price' attitude which is inevitably self-defeating. Whether or not Venus does bring good fortune is, of course, as with all the planets, determined by its position in the individual chart. As an astrologer I have also noticed that its effects vary considerably with the field-bandwidth or soul age of the individual. Love, it seems, means different things to different people!

## The Metaphysics:

The Greek Aphrodite was the classic, beautiful woman: fair haired, blue-eyed, voluptuous, Jung's 'Eve', the temptress and archetypal sex symbol or, as I have proposed in both *The Greek Tradition* and *Olympus*, the anima extravertedly expressed through the courtesan or *hetaira* mode.

And yet her attribute, the Girdle, seems somehow to deny much of this. So where does that lead us? Surely the message is that as far as humankind is concerned the Love Principle is expressed mostly at the carnal level, her son Eros, possibly by her husband Hephaestus or her lover Ares, depicting the kind of eroticism which would appear to be so blatantly the preference of the majority of hominids. So, while Aphrodite's dalliance with Ares (see Chapter 5, Mars) represents that which many of us are apt to refer to as 'love' but which is really 'lust', her legal union with Hephaestus (Vulcan) was of a higher order, having been engineered by Hera herself, Mother of the Gods, inferring intervention at a more exalted level. The symbology of her famous Girdle or Zona is surely telling us that pure love, at its very highest level, is the most powerful force in the Universe.

The story of Aphrodite's love for Adonis also appears in the Phoenician pantheon, a sure indication of its archetypal validity. Adonis is a Hellenized form of the Semitic word *Adōnai* – my Lord, my Master – which inclines me to think of this beautiful youth in terms of Aphrodite's animus. Adonis was killed by a wild boar or bear. An indication, perhaps, that Venus, at her higher Love Octave, dispensed with the lower or instinctive aspects of passion?

There are so many questions here that need answering, such as: what happened to Venus, the planet? Why have Venusian energies, if based on the fiery, inhospitable surface of Earth's planetary twin, become associated with such an exalted principle as spiritual love? Will she tell us? Let us see.

## The Dialogue:

V:   First of all, dear friend, let me tackle the physical side of my planet or, if you prefer, my soma. It all goes back a long, long way when Danuih and I, as close sisters, were both in line for the reception of certain species for the purpose of their evolution; while there was also a third member, thus creating the triad essential for the formation of matter with its alternating currents of order and chaos. It was decided that Danuih would take on the physical/instinctive role by providing habitation suitable for the evolution of a variety of species at that specific level, our male member would attend to the psychological/rational aspects of this growth program, which left me with the subtle/intuitive role. We each, therefore, adjusted our physical bodies accordingly and I, knowing that I was not destined to prepare my body to receive certain life-forms designated to evolve in this solar system, assisted by the Timeless Ones and the element of Fire, proceeded to effect the necessary adjustment. Danuih, also aided by the four elements but mainly that of Water, went about her business, which was to prepare herself to receive, among others, hominid-type beings, a species having strong water associations. However, in observing the minds of these beings, the third member of our party became aware that certain of them had, by their actions and inclinations, attracted a passing cosmic virus. In fact, he became so fascinated by the effect this virus had on its hosts, which was to give them a misguided sense of uniqueness and power and close their minds to the Ultimate Cosmic Reality that, instead of halting its spread, he actually encouraged it. As a result, he was forced to face the consequences of his actions which involved great upheavals on his surface and an unnatural polarity swing that was to have disastrous effects on the females of the hominid species for eons to come. The story is well represented in the many myths of humankind, not the least of which is the aforementioned tale of Michael and Lucifer, the end of which has still to be played out. Does this answer your question?

M: What can I say?

V: As for the Girdle, what the myth is telling you is, as you have suggested, that in order to attain to the higher octaves of the Love Principle one has to pass through the 'refining fire' of experience, as represented by my soma. Whereas the fires of my consort Vulcan are associated with the conversion of energy into matter as manifest via the archetypal Masonic principle, my somatic flames carry out the reverse in that they can transmute love from the level of matter to its higher frequencies, *providing one is ready to effect the transition from the carnal to the spiritual.* Much as I love you, dear one, I have experienced difficulty in finding adequate words in your data banks to express this information and have been obliged to rely on myth to an extent. But that is hardly your fault as you know the story as well as I do, but simply lack the terms of reference that would help me to render a more accurate account of what took place all those aeons ago and how it will all be resolved in the future.

M: I am SO sorry, Venus. I wish I was of more use to you.

V: Do not fret about it. I, too, am at fault in that I still have much
to learn. Knowing and appreciating your penchant for
archetypal correspondences you may wonder why neither
Vulcan nor I obliged in this respect. Well, the Adonis story
gives a clue as to my own and, as for Vulcan, you will need to
look no further than Ptah of Egypt. However, you must
appreciate that, in addition to the archetypal emphases, we are
all being constantly bombarded by a cocktail of cosmic
influences, many of which humankind would be totally
unfamiliar with. Besides, you must appreciate that the dual
characteristics you have been writing about are more
predominant in some planetary genii than others. When this,
my body, eventually dies and disintegrates, my next soma will
be a solar one, a young sun to be born in some far-flung area
of the Universe. But I shall sustain warm memories of my
sojourn in these parts. And now, dear one, be about your work
on the rest of this book and I offer you my Girdle of Protection.

M: I am deeply moved, Venus. Thank you so very much.

********

Endnotes:
(1) Musès, C. *The Lion Path*, p. 60.

Chapter 11

# COSMIC MESSENGERS, COURIERS, AND OTHER MINOR CELESTIAL PHENOMENA

In these chaotic times when PODS (prophets of doom), with increasing support from various branches of the scientific world, are having a heyday, our attention is naturally drawn to the type of celestial phenomena which could possibly herald the dreaded Doomsday. There is plenty to choose from – comets, asteroids, planetesimals being seen as possible culprits. It might help if we know what we are actually dealing with so here are a few definitions:

PLANETESIMALS:
Any of the innumerable small bodies consisting of interstellar dust thought to have been present in the presolar medium. In the planetesimal hypothesis, any of the innumerable small bodies thought to have been formed from gaseous solar material. The planetesimal hypothesis was put forward by T. C. Chamberlain and F. R. Moulton in 1906 to account for the formation of the planets in the solar system. It states that gas drawn off from the young Sun and another star as they passed close to each other condensed into planetesimals, which then by gravitation, aggregation and accretion formed the planets (ref. also nebular hypothesis and presolar nebular hypothesis).[1]
    The German scientist Otto Muck, when writing on the subject of Atlantis, speculated that a rogue planetesimal might well have caused the catastrophe which resulted in the pole shift and subsequent submergence of the Atlantic Ridge. But does this mean that such a

body could affect us similarly in the future? The majority of scientific researchers into the subject think not, comets or asteroids being more favoured as possible intruders.

## COMETS – MESSENGERS OF DOOM OR HOPE?:

A comet is a celestial body, observed only in that part of its orbit that is relatively close to the Sun, having a head consisting of a solid nucleus surrounded by a nebulous coma when sufficiently close to the Sun, and thought to consist chiefly of ammonia, methane, carbon-dioxide and water. (From the Greek:(*astēr*) *komētés*, 'Long Haired' [2]

Comets are probably the remnants of the nebula that formed the Sun and planets – lumps of rock and ice that are thought to orbit in a gigantic cloud that surrounds the solar system called the Oort Cloud. This cloud stretches from Neptune's orbit to around 2 light-years away and contains millions of comets in their frozen state. If a comet is knocked from its orbit towards the Sun, its fragments may be pulled in by Earth's gravity, or the gravity of any other planet for that matter, which was the case in the 1994 Jupiter phenomenon.

Meteorites, such as the Murchison meteorite found in Australia in 1969, can be identified as comet fragments because they contain water and carbon compounds. Comet-derived meteorites are of special interest to biologists because they carry traces of amino acids (the basis of all life-forms on Earth) that have been formed by non-living chemical processes.

Meteorites are also believed to have been derived from other planets in the solar system. For example, some, found mainly in Antarctica, have been identified as pieces of the Moon's surface while others, notably the Nakhla stone that fell in Egypt in 1911, are thought to have originated on Mars. Meteorites of this nature are created when another body such as an asteroid collides violently with the Moon or a planet, sending debris flying into space, some of which is captured by the Earth's gravity.

Comets are usually divided into two types, those with a short period which return regularly and the longer period variety whose periods range from hundreds to millions of years. Some comets are so affected by the gravity of larger planets that they are either changed to the short period mode or flung into parabolic paths which remove them from our view; Comet West, for example, which appeared in 1976, when it passed Jupiter after reaching perihelion.

The best known of these celestial wanderers is undoubtedly Halley's Comet, which seems to have captured the imagination of astronomers and mystics alike. It is known to have been observed as far back as 240 BC and possibly as early as 467 BC. However, it was not until 1682, when Edmund Halley noted that the comet of that year followed an identical orbit to those of 1607 and 1531, that he realized it to be one and the same body in each instance. Edmund Halley, incidentally, is probably best known among metaphysicists for the famous comment he evoked from Sir Isaac Newton when questioning the scientific basis for Newton's belief in astrology: 'Sir, I have studied it, you have not!'

THE HALLEY JINX:
The appearance of Halley's comet has long been associated with chaos of the kind that institutes change. Here are a few examples:

*87 BC.* – the ultimate death of the ancient Greek civilization when Athens fell to the Romans in the spring of that year.

*12 BC.* – when it was thought to signify the Star of Bethlehem which heralded the birth of Christ. However, it has recently emerged that this date is about five years too early, the 'star' probably referring to a conjunction of Jupiter and Saturn, or a possible supernova explosion somewhere else in the galaxy. (See Chapter 2.)

*66 AD.* – when the Comet's return was correlated with the Great Fire of Rome started, according to some, by the Emperor Nero himself.

*374 AD.* – when the Bible was translated into Latin by St. Jerome.

*451 AD.* –when its visitation was seen as the deciding factor in the battle between the Romans and Huns for control of Gaul.

*530 AD.* – when the Great Plague swept across Europe.

*837 AD.* – the invasion of London by the Vikings.

*1066 AD.* –the Battle of Hastings when William the Conqueror assumed the royal role of the defeated King Harold.

*1222 AD.* – the use of the first firebomb.

*1378.* – the Black Death, which was far worse than the 530 AD episode in that the death toll ran into millions.

1759 AD. – the conquest of Quebec.

These are just a few examples not, perhaps, as earth-shaking as might be imagined by modern-day PODS but obviously highly important to the eras in which they occurred.

However, we cannot blame all such untoward events on Halley's friend. Comet Arend-Roland appeared in 1957, a few weeks prior to the launch of Sputnik 1, the first artificial satellite to go into orbit around the Earth. Comet Kohoutek's appearance in 1973 coincided with the crisis in the oil industry which resulted in a whole new approach to the fuel factor worldwide, and the consequent investment in alternative forms of energy such as solar and wind power and, sadly, nuclear energy. While on the subject of nuclear power one cannot fail to observe that the Chernobyl disaster in April 1986 followed just days after Halley's Comet made its closest approach to Earth. So, is it any wonder that the advent of these celestial bodies is, and always has been, a cause for concern among many?

## THE TRANSPERMIA THEORY:
The eminent astronomer Fred Hoyle, writing in *The Intelligent Universe*, saw other uses for those celestial visitors we may either come to bless or dread. His theory of panspermia postulated the concept of microorganisms distributed throughout interspace which had already been considered by the British physicist Lord Kelvin during the nineteenth century. Hoyle tells us:

> 'Unfortunately, however, the possibility of understanding biological evolution here on the Earth in terms of this concept was not appreciated, with the consequence that scientists became forced away from what is almost surely the correct theory by the rising tide of Darwinism. This was in spite of the valiant effort early in the present century by the Swedish chemist Svante Arrhenius to support the "panspermia" theory, (meaning "seeds everywhere"), by carefully reasoned arguments.'[3]

When Hoyle's book was first published in 1983 there was still considerable opposition to the panspermia idea from biologists in particular. Doubtless Gribbin's book, from which I have quoted earlier, which combines the evolutionary theory with cosmology, would give the astronomer much to smile about, biologists, evolutionists and astro-physicists finally finding mutual ground for dialogue. Spores are undoubtedly carried through space via the many physical objects that travel around and through our solar system from time to time. These may be the stuff of which new 'bugs' are conceived, thus adding to mankind's increasing medical dilemmas, or they could equally provide triggers for those earlier discussed 'alleles' which designate the future survival of the human race.

While on this theme I am tempted to refer to an article sent to me recently from one of those burgeoning groups of American borderline-science publications which appear to engage in the occasional dalliance with New Age material. It concerned the effect of higher frequencies of light at both the subconscious and cellular levels, while also hinting at possible 'external' effects on our genes and chromosomes which could cause the DNA double helix to mutate by expanding from two strands to twelve! The stuff that science fiction is made of? Perhaps. But then perhaps not. Taking into account the escalating change in the climate of scientific opinion it behoves us, perhaps, to keep an open mind. After all, we might be dealing with Professor Hoyle's 'spores', or Dr. Gribbin's 'alleles'?

Meanwhile are there any possible culprits lurking on the cosmic horizon? According to *The Daily Mail* (July 31 1995), under the headline *Tale of a Comet that could spell disaster*, the report told of a huge object hurtling in our direction from outer space. Discovered by amateur astronomers in the U.S., and named Hale-Bopp, it was purported to have the appearance of a comet, its position at the time being well beyond Jupiter at the edge of the solar system, from where it could be seen with fairly small telescopes. Estimated by scientists as being about 1,000 miles wide, if a collision course were to occur it could easily extinguish life on Earth. The last news about it I could find was on 6th August, 1995, when it was reported as being beyond Jupiter in Scorpius, although some of my radio-listening friends have since told me of more recent news bulletins which suggest that it is proceeding safely (?) on its way!

The experts were careful to play down the disaster aspect, which proves fortunate in that later reports put minds at rest with the assurance that it would give our planet a wide berth. There were, however, some unanswered questions, Dr. Brian Marsden, of Harvard University, commenting, 'It is unheard of for a comet to be visible by small telescopes while so far away,' although he stressed that it could be a small comet that had suddenly brightened, meaning it gave off flares of gases that created an illusion of great size. The mystery deepens; or does it? After all, such phenomena have existed since time immemorial although it is only comparatively recently that we have been able to observe and compute them scientifically.

To quote an article which appeared in *The Times* shortly after the Jupiter impact:

> 'Catastrophe is suddenly back on the cast-list as an explanation of the past. Reputable scientists now dare suggest that some cosmic collision finished off classical civilisation and brought on the Dark Ages in Europe.
>
> 'Those infallible clocks that are buried in rocks and tree rings record a world disaster around AD 534, followed by a sudden slowing of tree growth in America and Europe lasting for about 15 years. Fallible human chronicles for the same date record that the Sun became dim for years.
>
> 'From China to Britain accounts survive of famine, pestilence, wars, crop failures and urban and economic decline. In parts of China the population suddenly decreased by 80 per cent, and in AD 534 the Chinese emperor ordered the half a million inhabitants to evacuate his imperial capital of Loyang for no recorded reason. In Constantinople the plague arrived and started the dwindling that was to reduce the population of the Byzantine imperial capital from 500,000 to 25,000.
>
> 'The evidence from both carbon-dating and chronicles points to massive pollution of the atmosphere and a kind of nuclear winter. No other natural disaster on record spread its ripples round the world in this way. A conventional interpretation of such evidence would be to postulate some vast volcanic eruption, like the one on Thera (Santorini) around 1,500 BC, which has been blamed for everything from the widespread legends of floods to the parting of the Red Sea for the Israelites and the sudden destruction of the Minoan civilisation. But Thera left its unmistakable signature on the ice cores dug from miles down in the Greenland ice-cap, which

plot the volcanic history of the planet for the past 9,000 years. These record no volcanic eruptions in the 530's.

'Some scientists now advance the theory that the worldwide cataclysm of 534 was caused by the impact of a giant meteor or fragments of a comet, like the pieces of Shoemaker-Levy that collided with Jupiter a week ago.* Although they have yet to identify a plausible footprint for such an earth-shaking crash, it could be under water or have been mistaken for the crater of a volcano.

'As an explanation for history or geology, catastrophe used to belong to the dark ages of superstition. For the past two centuries evolution has increasingly been seen as a uniform process in which everyday forces have shaped the Earth and the history of its inhabitants. Then it became scientifically respectable to speculate that dinosaurs were extinguished by some cosmic catastrophe. Now it turns out that the Dark Ages for humans may have been caused by some such collision with a comet. Next?'

*July 16th, 1995.

When it comes to the future of the Earth, however, of more concern than comets, as far as some experts are concerned, are asteroids.

ASTEROIDS:

Asteroids are described as any number of celestial bodies with characteristic diameters between one and several hundred miles and orbits lying in a zone, the *asteroid belt*, (see illustration page 142) chiefly between Mars and Jupiter. They are also referred to as 'minor planets' and 'planetoids'. Over the years there have been several metaphysical theories regarding the one-time existence of a planet in that area which subsequently blew up, although to my knowledge there is no astronomical evidence to support these.

A television programme in the 'Horizon' series entitled *Hunt for the Doomsday Asteroid*, transmitted by the BBC on 28 February 1994, caused much interest at the time. I missed it myself but subsequently sent for the text which I now have before me. The producer, Tim Haines, introduced the programme with the following comment:

'I first learnt about the idea of Earth being hit by a giant asteroid from a science-fiction film. But a year ago I heard that

NASA and the US Congress were seriously interested in the risk, and I couldn't resist looking deeper into the subject.

'It turned out that in the last few years a small group of short-sighted astronomers had been combing the space between the planets looking for cosmic rubble, and they had found rather a lot of it. Strange-shaped rocks on chaotic orbits – dead comets, metal asteroids and clusters of rocks rolling round and round each other. Their work triumphed recently with the observation of Shoemaker-Levy 9 – the train of glowing mountains that is just about to smash into Jupiter with the energy of billions of Hiroshima bombs.

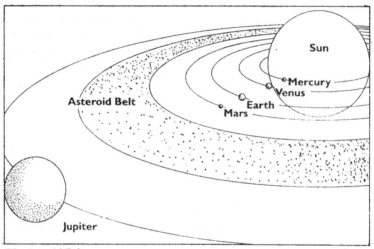

*The Asteroid Belt*

'The programme I have made looks at the difficulty in accepting the implications of this work – that one day Earth will be hit. We are used to doomsday predictions from mystics and science-fiction writers, but how do we cope when science supports the idea? It is also easy to imagine huge Earth-threatening explosions but when we are told they might only arrive at ten-million-year intervals, how do we imagine that? Behind the whole subject is the appreciation of risk – the Earth will be hit one day but for you and me the car is far, far more dangerous.'

For those interested in the programme's full content, which included contributions from top scientists such as Gene Shoemaker of

Shoemaker-Levy fame, the ensuing text – an adaptation, not a verbatim reproduction of the programme as transmitted – is available from BBC Education for BBC Horizon.

ASTEROIDS IN ASTROLOGY:
In recent years, certain asteroids in particular have come to play a more active role in astrology. These have been classified as 'major' and 'minor', the major ones being Juno, Pallas, Vesta and Ceres; and the minor, Psyche, Eros, Lilith, Toro, Sappho, Amor, Pandora, Icarus, Diana, Hidalgo, Urania and Chiron. With the exception of Toro and Hidalgo, all of these have been named after characters from Greek mythology. So why Toro, and who was Hidalgo? Toro is, of course, the Spanish word for bull, and as such the asteroid thus named is believed to represent the principle of boundless strength and power. Hidalgo, on the other hand, was named after Miguel Hidalgo y Costilla, the father of Mexican Independence, born into the Spanish upper class in 1753. As a Catholic priest and revolutionary he worked to improve the economic conditions of his impoverished Indian parishioners. He was captured, tried, excommunicated, and shot as a rebel on July 31, 1811.

As this book goes to print, a new planetoid has been discovered by British amateur astronomer, George Sallit. Provisionally named 'Sallit One', it is approximately 200 million miles from Earth. Details were sent to America's Smithsonian Institution via the computer Internet, and Mr. Sallit learned his find was authentic in an e-mail message from the American space agency NASA. Although the planetoid is probably only ten miles across, it is still viewed as an important find in the world of astronomy. I will be interested to see what astrologers make of this one and, since I believe there to be no such thing as coincidence, the nature of the timely, and doubtless appropriate subtle energies it will be casting upon our woeful sphere.

For those interested in the astrology of asteroids there is an excellent book on the subject by Demetra George, who also provides a comprehensive Ephemeris of the placings of the major four from 1931 to the year 2000. But for the vaguely curious only I will give a few condensed details.

## THE FOUR MAIN ASTEROIDS;

JUNO:          The Divine Consort – relatedness.
PALLAS:        The Warrior Queen – creative wisdom and
                   androgyny.
VESTA:         The Eternal Flame – focus and commitment.
CERES:         The Mother Principle of Unconditional Love.

## THE MINOR ASTEROIDS:

PSYCHE:        The capacity to be physically sensitive to another
                   person.
EROS:          The capacity  for vitality and passion.
LILITH:        The capacity to release constructively repressed
                   anger and resolve conflict.
TORO:          The capacity to use and control power.
SAPPHO:        The capacity for romantic and artistic sensitivity.
AMOR:          The capacity for spiritual or platonic love and
                   compassion.
PANDORA:       The capacity for curiosity which initiates change.
ICARUS:        The capacity for liberation and risk-taking.
DIANA:         The capacity for survival and self-protection.
HIDALGO:       The capacity for self-assertion in defence of
                   principles.
URANIA:        The capacity for inspired knowledge.
CHIRON:        The capacity for wholistic understanding.[4]

For me, the most important of these is Chiron. Discovered in 1977
by astronomer Charles Kowal, Chiron is described as 'a planetoid
rather than an asteroid', travelling between the orbits of Saturn and
Uranus. The myth of Chiron the Healer is featured in detail in my
*Olympus*, and in *Practical Greek Magic*, in which I explained the cosmic
origins of those strange beings designated Tutors to the Gods. But
suffice it to say such mythological beings are not of this world or
solar system, their origins being on a small planet with two moons
which the Satyrs and Centaurs shared with the fabulous Unicorns.
Magical eyewash? Hardly! Astronomers believe that Chiron the
planetoid originated outside our solar system and will eventually
leave it. Likewise the mythological Chiron came from another
realm and left humankind to return to his own domains after he had

completed his teachings. Chiron featured in my earlier-mentioned references to Hercules, a wound he sustained proving so painful that he forfeited his immortality to the Hero so that, by experiencing death, he could be relieved of his pain. All highly symbolic, of course. For his sacrifice, Zeus set him in the heavens as the constellation of Sagittarius which tells us quite clearly from which neck of the cosmic woods his people originated!

Chiron has a 49-year orbit which is believed to symbolize the number of higher wisdom (7 x 7), so venerated by the Essenes (among other ancient sects) that they kept every fiftieth day (Pentecost) as a feast-day. His students included Achilles, Jason, and the healer Asclepius, later designated the Greek god of Medicine and believed to correspond to the Egyptian godling healer Nefer-Tem, son of Ptah and Sekhmet.

Chiron is the only one of the asteroids to which I feel particularly drawn, but then he has been associated with the rulership of Virgo so, as a Virgoan, I am tempted to see if he would honour me with a few words of knowledge and advice.

## The Dialogue:

M: Chiron, may I converse with you?

C: And so our paths cross once more as we proceed on our cosmic journeys of instruction and learning. I am delighted that you have made this contact. So, what can I do for you this time?

M: You remind me of other requests I have made to you for advice concerning healing and other matters. In this context I feel something of a 'taker'. Please forgive.

C: There is nothing to forgive. May I remind you of your conversation with Silenus in the garden some years back in Earth time? You were helpful to both of us on that occasion, as you will recall, so we are only exchanging energies, as is ever the case between our kind and the Time Essences.

M: As you know, dear friend, healing plays an important role among humankind. Are there any tips you can give my readers

regarding the direction that the study and application of this
service might take in the future?

C:   The transformations will be drastic, to say the least. Technology
will flourish to a certain point and then – Bang! The nuts and
bolts will no longer be available and the *actual* will slowly give
way to the *virtual*. As the planet changes direction so will the
surrounding energy fields adjust accordingly. You have already
cited incidents of how extra-terrestrial phenomena have affected
the health and mortality of all creatures extant on Danuih's
body in the past. Add several 'noughts' to the equation and you
will get a clearer picture of the highly radical nature of the
mutations that are destined to take place, especially in the area
of genetics. For example, one simple genetic adjustment could
eradicate aggression, cruelty, rape, murder, and a host of other
antisocial maladies which tend to afflict hominid males in
particular. Humankind as a species tends to place too much
emphasis on its fragile mortality; but there will come a time in
the future history of the human race when people will vacate
their bodies without the stress and pain of serious illness. They
will simply know when their time has come, be it long or short,
and will handle their affairs accordingly without fear or regret.
Likewise, those suffering the loss of loved ones will also
understand and feel glad rather than sad in the knowledge that
such transitions are a normal part of those comings and goings
in the cosmos which form the byways of evolution.

M:   Thank you, Chiron. Oh, and one more question. Does everyone
**possess healing skills? I hear certain New Age people suggesting
that these skills lie dormant in all hominids, and can therefore
be surfaced by undertaking a few courses or seminars?**

C:   I fear that those who attend such courses are sadly misguided
by their egos, while those who arrange them are either genuinely
ignorant of Cosmic Law or more concerned with their Bank
Accounts than the effect such beliefs may have on gullible
young fields (souls). May I put it to you (and them) this way: is
everyone a great artist, singer, mathematician, surgeon, etc.?
Of course not. Each member of the human race is blessed with
certain gifts which the field has deemed essential for negotiation

in its present human existence. These gifts, or frequency-negotiabilities as I prefer to call them, differ considerably with the individual. As to healing abilities, as you would say, the proof of the pudding inevitably lies in the eating. The ability to self-heal is something that eventually comes with the expansion of the field bandwidth, or spiritual maturity if you prefer, the truly wise person knowing exactly when to make use of this faculty and when the time has come to let go and pass on. As I see it, one of the problems with healing in your world today is that it has become too compartmentalized. The surgeon is separated from the general practitioner, the medical profession as a whole from complementary medicine and alternative therapies, and so on. Of course there are those people who are able to effect the healing process because the nature of their field is such that it can channel certain cosmic frequencies, via the brain, which can assist in the balancing of chaos/order factors in human (and other) bodies. The genuinely gifted healer does this instinctively, without the need for quick-sale weekend seminars and the like, while there are many among the medical profession itself who do it naturally, every day, and not necessarily via the prescriptions they are expected to hand out. So, although study and practical experience can obviously improve performance, healers, my dear friend, are, like good doctors, good teachers, and good psychics/occultists, born, not 'bought' or 'made'.

M: Thank you, Chiron. That one is, I fear, going to put the proverbial cat among the pigeons, but I have no intention of watering it down to please certain elements in society.

C: Good, and now a final word of advice, prompted by your reference to pigeons. There are, among the animal world, many skilled healers. Cats, in particular, can help the mentally afflicted, so can fish, while among dogs and horses there are those who carry out their corrective skills in more practical ways. Think about it. And yes, my Virgo friend, I have been assisting Mercury to influence your sign and will continue to do so until such time as Vulcan takes over. And on that note I will bid you a fond adieu.

*******

**Endnotes:**

(1) *Readers Digest Great Illustrated Dictionary*, Vol. 2, p. 1299.

(2) *Ibid.*, Vol. 1, p. 351.

(3) Hoyle, F. *The Intelligent Universe*, p. 158.

(4) George, Demetra. *The Asteroid Goddesses*, p. 18.

Chapter 12

# THE SUN

Throughout this book I have referred to the Sun in the feminine rather than the masculine mode favoured by most astrologers and metaphysicists. As I have already covered the explanation for this in previous chapters, only a brief summary is called for at this point. All celestial bodies, in keeping with all creation, carry the potential for both the negative (receptive/passive) and positive (outgoing/active) modes. As the evolutionary gap closes and the field (soul) attains to the higher frequencies, these two aspects slowly fuse together to create the androgyn. Until that time, however, those fields that have individuated from the collective in which they originated (see Chapter 13) may work on either side of the polarity as suits the occasion. So, although astrology is unanimous in its insistence on a masculine Sun the planets, it seems, think otherwise. But, as far as humankind is concerned, the positive aspect is obviously more acceptable to the male-orientated cultures of today's civilizations. So, while favouring the planetary stance, as far as I am concerned I am happy to respect both views.

## Astronomical Data:
Our Sun is, by definition, a star. A star is formed out of clouds of gas and dust after which it joins the main sequence for up to 10,000 million years. After that it becomes a red giant during which phase it grows brighter and larger until it finally becomes unstable and begins to eject its outer layers. Eventually it collapses into a white dwarf and its glow fades.

As our closest star, the Sun is our lifeline to the Universe. Described as a 'thermonuclear furnace in the sky', it is a vast globe of incandescent gas that provides the light and heat upon which all life on Earth depends. In the Universe, however, it is merely an average star which appears extra large and bright only because it is so much closer. Although the Sun has a mass 330,000 times greater than the Earth it would have burned out millions of years ago if it blazed in the same way as wood or coal. In fact, the Sun generates its power by the fusion process in which energy is created as the heat at its core turns hydrogen gas into helium. It will continue radiating more energy per second than man has ever used or will ever use for aeons to come.

The Sun has a mean distance from Earth of about 150 million kilometres (93 million miles) and a diameter of approximately 1.39 million kilometres (865,000 miles). Its body consists of a radiation zone, from which heat travels outwards from atom to atom, a photosphere which is its visible surface, a convection zone from which heat rises in large gas masses by convection, a chromosphere – a layer of gas 1600-4800 kilometres (1,000-3,000 miles) thick – and a core or nuclear furnace converting hydrogen to helium at 15,000,000 degrees Centigrade. Other features include solar prominences (arches of incandescent gas), sunspots (paths of cooler gas on the surface) and solar flares (violent eruptions of energy). Outermost is its Corona or surrounding halo of light which extends millions of miles into space.

As a nuclear reactor, its dense, intensely hot core gives out most of its energy in the form of X-rays which seep out to heat the surrounding material. By the time it reaches the surface the radiation has given way to convection. It takes about thirty million years for light generated in the core to reach the Earth. Escaping energy makes the Sun's outer region seethe and gyrate, some of the gigantic flares that shoot out in this dramatic boiling-off process dwarfing the Earth.[1]

So say the official text-books. But things, it seems, are changing even on the Sun itself, with new evidence suggesting that the Earth is entering a period of maximum earthquake activity triggered by the combined effect of peak solar winds and minimum sunspots. An alarming article in the magazine *Nexus* (April/May 1995), an Australian publication, gives details of recent findings concerning the Sun's apparently unusual behaviour over the last 400 years.

Quoting firstly from an earlier article in the Dec.92/Jan.93 issue, writer Stan Deyo tells us:

'... there is a growing debate in various scientific circles as to whether or not the Sun is actually shrinking at the moment. One of the main proponents of such a theory is astronomer John Eddy of the Center for Astrophysics at the High Altitude Observatory at Boulder, Colorado, in the USA.'

Eddy, it seems, certainly attracted a lot of support for the work he and his co-worker, Aram Boornazian, have done on the shrinking solar diameter theory.

'Eddy and Boornazian researched astronomical data from as far back as 1567 AD to find that there was no doubt that the diameter of the Sun is smaller than it was then. To their surprise, they found that the US Naval Observatory in Washington had been keeping records which agreed with their data from at least 1840 AD forward (see Chart No. 1 Solar Diameter changes 1840-1950). Their data showed the Sun has truly been shrinking at the rate of 16 kilometres per year. Were that shrinkage to continue at the same linear rate for another 96,000 years, the Sun would no longer exist.

'On 31st July this year (1992), Dr. Robert Jastrow, who formerly headed the prestigious Goddard Institute of Space Studies for 20 years and who now directs the George C. Marshall Institute which specialises in defence and environmental issues, stated that global warming may be due to changes in the Sun rather than to the so-called "Greenhouse Effect".

'If the Sun is shrinking it may reach a point where it will collapse into a smaller star complete with a different spectral emission signature. In the process, it may produce violent magnetic field changes, massive shifts in the solar wind density, changes in the orbits of the planets and may even cause the ejection of its current surface layer as a "cooler" fragmented shell of matter into the orbits of the inner planets. This could cause changes in the light levels from the Sun as well as changes in the visible solar spectrum, which might even cause the colour of the Moon to change for a short time. Debris may actually hit the Earth should the outer solar shell blow off; and the Earth may be moved to sway on its own axis due to solar gravitational changes.'

Viewing the aforementioned (1992) information in the light of current knowledge Deyo comments:

'The Sun has been shrinking, and for some undisclosed reason the ozone layer is now weakening to the point that UV penetration is a serious health hazard to all who dwell on the Earth's surface. Are the two phenomena linked? I must also point out that even though the diameter of the Sun has been decreasing on Chart No. 1, I have just received an as yet unconfirmed report that the solar diameter has increased by over one hundred kilometres in the last two years. If indeed this proves correct, then something extraordinary may be on the way.'

As the article goes on for several pages, those interested can obtain a copy from Nexus, PO Box 71, Kalamunda WA 6076, Australia. Included is a chart of earthquake activity from 1963 to 1993 as equated with sunspot activity, which is also reproduced under.

## Earthquakes;

Earthquakes, as we know, occur where the great rigid plates that form the crust of the Earth jostle and push against each other. The junction of two such plates is called a 'fault-line'. Being a native of, and resident in the British Isles I am constantly being asked whether there are any major fault-lines here and, if so, where? Fortunately, earthquakes in the British Isles are comparatively rare, so here is a motley collection of data from both ancient records and the British Geological Survey in Edinburgh:

The English Chronicle states that in 1089 there came 'a mickle earth-stirring all over England' while, according to the Chronicle of Florence of Worcester, in 1110 the bed of the River Trent was dry for a whole morning after a tremor. In the great quake of 1185 Lincoln Cathedral was complete destroyed, while in 1247 an English Monk named Matthew Paris, recorded a considerable earthquake throwing down buildings in London and causing the tide to cease for three months.

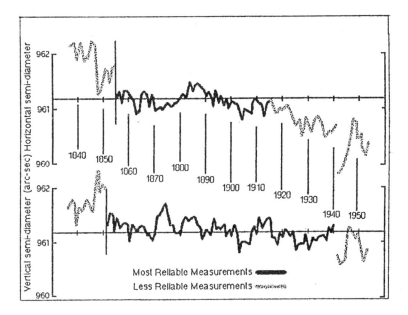

Solar Diameter Changes 1840 - 1950

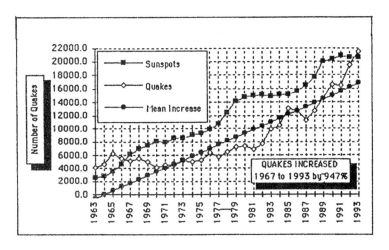

Global Earthquakes 1963 - 1993

In 1246 or 1248, depending on the reference, the tower of Wells Cathedral was felled and churches throughout the region were damaged, but the worst disturbance of all occurred in 1275, with churches and houses being destroyed all over the land. On August 13, 1816, a tremor shook Aberdeen so strongly that it threw people out of bed and damaged much of the town. It was felt throughout Scotland.

In more recent times, however, the most severe British quake on June 7, 1931, measured 6 on the Richter scale. With an off-shore epicentre near Dogger Bank the worst effects were avoided and minor damage occurred along the east coast only. The most severe, in terms of damage, was on April 22, 1884, with an epicentre just south of Colchester and magnitude estimated at 4.6. It caused considerable damage to villages in the area, bringing down many chimneys and roof tiles and leaving buildings with large wall cracks. Shock waves from the 1884 Colchester earthquake were felt over an area of 53,000 square miles  as far away as Exeter in Devon and Ostend in Belgium. The strongest Welsh tremor occurred in Swansea in June 1906 and was felt across 37,800 miles, while a shock in north Wales on July 19, 1984, stopped traffic lights in Dublin!

By comparison, the recent earthquake at Kobe, in Japan (1995), measured 6.9 on the Richter scale so, while we may not suffer from the wrath of Danuih and her Mother as much as other nations, we had still better watch our p's and q's as far as our terrestrial host and her parent are concerned!

## A Solar Seeker:

A tiny spacecraft named Ulysses has recently been supplying some interesting information regarding the solar effects on weather worldwide. Moving at 95,000 mph it has been monitoring the solar wind, a stream of particles travelling at supersonic speed which carry its magnetism towards the Earth. Ulysses has become the first craft to explore the polar regions of the Sun after using the gravitational strength of Jupiter to reach an orbit beyond the range of any man-made launcher. John Simpson, professor of physics at the University of Chicago, put forward the idea of sending a space-probe to the Sun's poles in 1959, two years after the first Sputnik flight, and has participated in more than thirty years of planning for Ulysses, named after the hero in Dante's *Inferno* who set his sights on 'the uninhabited world behind the sun'. Let us hope that this dauntless cosmic traveller provides us with some of the answers to our many questions regarding our solar friend.

Shedding new light on the Sun

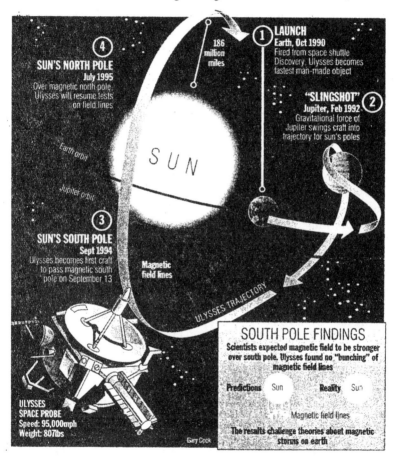

**LAUNCH**
**Earth, Oct 1990**
Fired from space shuttle Discovery, Ulysses becomes fastest man-made object

**"SLINGSHOT"**
**Jupiter, Feb 1992**
Gravitational force of Jupiter swings craft into trajectory for sun's poles

**SUN'S NORTH POLE**
**July 1995**
Over magnetic north pole, Ulysses will resume tests on field lines

**SUN'S SOUTH POLE**
**Sept 1994**
Ulysses becomes first craft to pass magnetic south pole on September 13

186 million miles

Earth orbit

Jupiter orbit

SUN

Magnetic field lines

ULYSSES TRAJECTORY

**ULYSSES SPACE PROBE**
Speed: 95,000mph
Weight: 807lbs

Gary Cook

**SOUTH POLE FINDINGS**
Scientists expected magnetic field to be stronger over south pole. Ulysses found no "bunching" of magnetic field lines

Predictions    Sun          Reality    Sun

Magnetic field lines

The results challenge theories about magnetic storms on earth

## The Myth:

Mythology abounds with solar references, some of which relate to suns other than our own: the Egyptian story of Ra, for example, which I am convinced refers to the collapsed star Sirius B. However, having written extensively on this subject in *The Sirius Connection, The*

*Lion People*, and several other of my earlier books, rather than take up valuable space herein I would refer those interested to the above, all of which are available in the Public Lending Library system.

In Greek mythology the Sun was represented by more than one character. Apollo was its primary deity – the spirit, or light, of the Sun – while the visible body was allotted to Helios. The Greek cult of Helios was very ancient and was practised throughout the land, at Elis, Apollonia, on the Acropolis of Corinth, at Argos, at Troezen, on Cape Raenarum, at Athens, in Thrace and, especially, in the Island of Rhodes which was sacred to him. In Rhodes could be seen a colossal statue of Helios, the renowned work of the sculptor Chares. It was about thirty yards high, and ships in full sail could pass between the god's legs. The story told how Helios was drowned in the ocean by his uncles, the Titans, and then raised to the sky, where he became the luminous sun. Every morning Helios emerged in the east, riding in the golden chariot fashioned for him by Hephaestus, which was drawn by winged horses; these were of dazzling white, their nostrils breathed fire, and the names were Lampon, Phaethon, Chronos, Aethon, Astrope, Bronte, Pyroeis, Eous and Phlegon.

One of Helios's sons, Phaeton, was to leave his particular mark on the solar story. A dispute arose among the gods as to Phaeton's claim to immortality, as a result of which he begged a favour from his father which would prove to all eyes that he was indeed the son of the Sun God. Helios gave his promise and swore it by the River Styx, which made the oath irrevocable. Phaeton then demanded permission to drive the Sun's chariot for one day. In vain his father tried to dissuade the presumptuous youth from his insane project, but Phaeton insisted and Helios was bound by his oath. The horses, however, no longer restrained by the firm hand of their usual driver, rushed wildly through space, carrying the unhappy Phaeton, who had completely lost control, with them. The chariot came too near the Earth, as a result of which the rivers dried up and the soil began to burn. In fact the universe would have been destroyed by flame had not Zeus struck the rash youth with a thunderbolt and sent him tumbling into the waters of the Eridanus. He was buried by the kindly mymphs.[2]

Now is it my imagination or does this tale not have a familiar ring about it? As I have said all through this book, the myths refer *not just to the past but also to the present and the future.* Perhaps we are being told that the masculine aspect of the Sun (Phaeton?) will give way to the feminine (Earth being a watery planet?) *following the advent of certain events destined to take place within this solar system.* I was intrigued to note the reference to the possible destruction of 'the universe', which immediately placed the Zeus character in the story among the universal archetypes rather than the planetary, solar or galactic genii. The original drowning of Helios could be seen to refer to the sinking of Atlantis and subsequent incorporation of the Atlantean solar deity into the ranks of the many divinities of the surviving world.

**Astrology:**
Solar key-words favoured by modern astrologers include power, vitality and self-expression. The type of person showing solar characteristics is seen as magnanimous, proud, regal, vital, warm, dignified and generous, the flip-side to these virtues being arrogance, despotism, domineering, extravagance, pomposity, profligation, and an overbearing and autocratic nature. I have also noticed that a well placed and aspected Sun tends towards good health and an active immune system.

Astrologers inevitably cast the Sun in the masculine role and the Moon in the feminine; thus, when charts are compared for compatibility factors (synastry), Sun/Moon contacts are seen as important. In heliocentric (Sun-centred) astrology, heliocentric coordinates refer to planetary placings *as seen from the Sun's centre,* with all the planets circling around her. In this system the Earth is always exactly opposite the natal Sun, so perhaps that is how the Solar Mother sees us?

# THE METAPHYSICS:

My contacts with the Paschats and 'Crystal People' (an appellation I have come to dislike on the grounds that they have been seen as having some association with the New Age crystal craze, which could not be farther from the truth) refer to our Sun as the child of Sirius meaning, of course, the result of some reaction between the Sirius 'A' we now view in our night skies and the collapsed Sirius 'B', which went supernova aeons ago. All seed stars, they insist, are predominantly feminine, so Danuih's original reference to the Sun as her Mother and the Sirius stars as her grandparents makes metaphysical sense. Of course I cannot prove any of this but then how many metaphysical truths can stand up in the light of logic? What we have to do is to bide our time until the appropriate 'discoveries' are made, after which the science fiction becomes the science fact and the myth the reality. And happen it will.

In the final chapter of this book which was, as I have explained, written prior to Chapters 11 and 12, the Spirit of the Universe has described to me how negative/passive universes are seeded by passing positive/active universes, the 'mothers' inevitably giving birth, in the fullness of cosmic time, to the next critical mass destined to make its noisy entrance into matter via the Big Bang of birth. For the time being we must therefore assume that the same principle applies to binary seed stars like Sirius A and B. But what of our own Sun? Perhaps her thoughts on these matters might serve to throw some light on this enigma, whereupon I shall hand over to she whom her planetary charges elect to address as 'Mother'.


## The Dialogue:

S:  I pre-empt your mental request, so let us proceed with those questions I see, through your eyes, written on your reference pad.

M:  The first question comes from a scientist friend who asks for your views on the complexity/reductionist debate.

S:  I observe that some of your scientists are so obsessed with the policy of reductionism that they fail to see the broader picture. Were they to marry the two as it were, and seek confirmation of their findings in complexity, the answers would be obvious. What we are basically dealing with here is the microcosm and the macrocosm. But since one inevitably reflects the other, debate is pointless. There will always be those scientists who like to approach problems from the 'bottom end' and seek their information at the microcosmic level, and those who prefer to seek outwardly in the cosmos. They will both come up with the same results in the end.

M: Any comments, please, on all the earlier mentioned material regarding changes in your body?

S: Of course my body is changing. It always has done and always will do. These changes occur in cycles – sometimes I may appear to shrink, others to expand; these are but my inbreathings and outbreathings. Will they affect the body of Danuih? – That is really what you want to know. Of course they will. But then the whole solar system is due for a radical change and I will naturally play my part in restoring balance among my 'family'. However, I do not anticipate reducing my mass in the manner suggested earlier ('collapsing into a smaller star with a different spectral emission signature'). As for my playing a role in the 'Greenhouse Effect', Dr. Jastrow is correct in part. You see, there are several contributors to this factor and, as Danuih explained to you in your earlier book, these changes are by no means due entirely to your industrial effluent. Carbon dioxide in the air controls your climate: the more of it in the air, the hotter the planet becomes. Danuih, with *my help*, is accelerating the heat process as she is anxious to rid herself of her illness. The time will come when the fever will break. That time will be crucial for all creatures extant on Danuih's body. There will be, as you have been told, those who survive and those who do not. Humankind always look after their own. Likewise do we, the planetary and solar genii, look after ours. When there is a clash of interest, such as exists at present on your planet, humankind cannot hope to win, the odds stacked against them being far too high. And yet there are those who rightly belong on Danuih's body and I, and the rest of my 'family', will ensure that these survive to inherit the Golden Age which is justly theirs.

M: Thank you, Mother Sun. And may I ask, on behalf of my friends who love you and your planetary family, do you prefer to be known in the feminine or, as the astrologers would have it, in the masculine?

S: For now, and over the ensuing epochs, I would prefer the feminine. In time, however, when humankind has long departed from the body of Danuih, the positive or active side of my nature will take over in preparation for my own, final demise.

M: Scientists speak of a new form of supremely violent energy that has been identified in the Universe, the 'gamma ray bursters'. These are said to occur when two super-dense neutron stars crash into each other at close speed. Most stars, unlike you are, it seems, partners in double star systems. In some rare cases, scientists tell us, both of these stars could be six times heavier than you. In this case they will both — at different times — explode as supernovae leaving, as remnants, objects so dense that a thimbleful of their material weighs more than 10,000 million tons?

S: It always amuses me when Earth scientists come out with these amazing 'discoveries', as though they were a fairly recent phenomena performing solely for their benefit. Such things have existed since the birth of the Universe, and will continue to do so until her demise. Nothing ever remains static. Change is continual. There are nuclear forces in our galaxy, the nature and energy of which would amaze your scientists. As these are slowly located and analyzed, each will pale in the light of later discoveries. As far as the collision of neutron stars is concerned there is little humankind can do about it anyway, other than to heed their own, minuscule role in the whole creative process and, hopefully, learn humility from it. The Cosmos — and that goes for all of us 'out here' — would be far more kindly disposed to humankind if it were a little more kindly disposed towards us, and the other poor, unfortunate life-forms with which it shares the shelter of Danuih's body. When humankind learns to treat its animals, trees, elements, minerals, etc. with kindness, acknowledging their existence as conscious entities, and carrying out its true role as carers of these complementary life forms, then we cosmic Beings might, perhaps, return the compliment.

M: Time-travel, it seems has been accepted as a future reality, although there has been some debate among scientists as to whether this would allow people to alter their own past by murdering their ancestors or even preventing their own birth. Your comments, please?

S:  Your scientists still have much to learn regarding the nature of Time. For example, there is a point in the Time Spectrum at which all Time exists simultaneously. As the scale descends, it undergoes a gradual slowing-down process, the frequencies of which are dictated by the density of the encountered mass. Therefore, familiarity with the correct coordinates are prerequisite to the accessing of those points on the Time-scale that represent Danuih's past. Fortunately, the Universe in which we all live is supplied with a goodly selection of time-tunnels in the form of Wormholes and Black holes, each of which is designed to serve as an access point into, and out of, the Time Spectrum. There are, however, certain basic laws governing the manipulation of Time, the breaking of which, albeit through ignorance, can produce strange, and somewhat frightening effects. For example, time travellers returning to the past with the specific idea of changing their ancestry, world events, or whatever, could find themselves automatically catapulted into a parallel universe in which the alterations they have in mind *already exist*. However, following events destined to take place in my system in the future, help and advice in these matters will be readily available from enlightened sources external to your own world.

M:  While on the subject of Time, during my conversations with the Universe, she indicated that visits to your planetary system by the Timeless Ones are somewhat rare. No doubt you are familiar with this, so I have been requested to ask you for your stance in the matter.

S:  There is nothing I can add to her comment. However, for the benefit of your readers generally, I can confirm that my system has been visited by one of the Timeless Ones, whom Danuih has already mentioned, who was accompanied originally by five young Time Essence trainees (described by Danuih as 'progeny'), all of whom have subsequently taken human form for some specific purpose. And this covers the whole history of your planet. Incidentally, the number five is important to the Time Beings, their trainees usually travelling to different systems in groups of five. It is a cosmic law that we protect these beings while they wear human, alien, or animal bodies, although we are precluded from showing them any favours. The likelihood of the majority of people ever meeting one is therefore remote, and it is only by their specific area of knowledge that they would be recognizable to those with 'eyes' to see! The evolutionary status of such beings has nothing to do with the 'old soul/ Master' syndrome I hear bandied about so liberally among your esotericists. I regret to inform you that the number of genuine 'old souls', or fields with bandwidths sufficiently wide to negotiate Universes beyond the one which houses my soma, is infinitesimal. And as for the rubbish we hear talked about 'ascended masters' and the like, all I can say on behalf of myself and my solar family is 'enjoy your ego trips while you may, for the awful hour of truth is about to dawn when humankind, both singly and collectively, will be forced to view itself in true perspective'.

M: At the purely human level I have been requested to ask you if there is anything that can be done to help errant teenagers whose period of chaos has gone 'over the top'?

S: With so much adverse energy about on your planet is it any wonder that those who are young in body and field (soul) are unable to control themselves? Besides, modern society seems to delight in feeding these ravenously chaotic appetites with a diet of self destruction. All part of the 'winding down' process of accelerated chaos, I regret to say. But then there are many teenagers who do manage to cope with their hormonal chaos. While on the subject of the hominid collective there is one point I would like to make. All collectives contain the elements of both chaos and order, both divisions having their extremes, these being easily identifiable in human society. Those hominids who have not as yet individuated from the collective – and this covers the majority – are inclined to express the orderly principle via the 'stability mode', and the chaotic principle via the 'rebellious mode', with the orderly tending to condemn the chaotic, and the chaotic to despise the orderly. Both close ranks, however, against those who do not appear to fit into either category. The individuated psyche, on the other hand, runs neither with 'the hare nor the hound', electing to steer a central and personally unique path which, while acknowledging the existence of both 'sides', favours neither.

M: The final question I have been asked to put to you concerns the subject of 'angels'. Russian cosmonauts are reputed to have seen such creatures and they have apparently been sighted by astronauts during space missions, one astronaut actually claiming that such a 'being' followed him back to Earth! Eyewash or fact?

S: Nature, as your scientists well know, abhors a vacuum. What you refer to as 'space' is therefore occupied by many forms of life, the majority of which would be totally unfamiliar to you. These range from minute particles to Essences of other evolutionary streams who also have their duties to perform. I note that these angelic beings are supposed to live within my system. May I hasten to assure all that they are by no means limited to my meagre domains. What humans refer to as 'angels' are a specialized body of Beings, whose ranks can be subdivided. Their natural 'home' is within the elemental kingdoms, being part of that evolutionary sub-structure. Angels, if you must refer to them as such, are not all 'angels', however. There are as many angels of chaos as there are of order. But then such knowledge exists in human arcane tradition and I would ask you, little friend, to outline this for the benefit of those among your readers who feel more comfortable if things are pigeonholed for them. May I add a final word: as regards the 'visions' witnessed by the astronauts and cosmonauts, the human brain inevitably converts unfamiliar energy-forms/ intelligences into structures, or figures with which it is conversant. In other words, we are back to the software again. People whose software carries a Christian, Judaic, Islamic or similarly related program, when confronted by an alien intelligence, are more than likely to convert that energy-source into an angelic picture. Likewise the followers of the UFO cult, who invariably 'see' aliens every time they encounter the unfamiliar! I do seem to be putting a damper on many cherished views, don't I! However, apologize I will not. I have been asked for advice and, as Leader of this solar system I must render such information as I possess in accordance with my knowledge of the goings-on therein.

M: Thank you, Mother. Here is the information you asked for. Angels are described in our dictionaries as: 'Immortal or spiritual Beings, attendant on God, conventionally represented as winged beings of human form. In medieval angelology, there are nine of these Orders of spiritual beings (listed from the highest to the lowest): Seraphim, Cherubin, Thrones, Dominations (or Dominions), Virtues, Powers, Principalities, Archangels and Angels. A guardian spirit or guiding influence.'

According to arcane tradition the angelic 'choirs' are associated with the elemental forces thus: the Seraphim, Virtues and Powers are of a fiery character, the Cherubin terrestrial, the Thrones and Archangels aquatic, and the Dominations and Principalities are aeriel. There is a 'Dictionary of Angels' available on the Public Library circuits while, for the collector of antiquities, Burton's *Anatomy of Melancholy* and Heywoods' *Hierarchy of the Blessed Angels* may both be consulted. For Christian readers, of course, the works of St. Thomas Aquinas, known as The Angelic Doctor, also provides a source of information on the more orthodox concepts of these beings.

S: May I please be allowed the final word? Love is a Universal Principle that can only operate successfully in a *self-disciplined* and caring environment. I have love for all those creatures that dwell within my domains but I am also aware of their failings. This love I have is not limited to any one aspect of creation – for me, as with the Universe herself and all my other planetary children – it is distributed equally to ALL. In withholding love and acknowledgement to *all* other life-forms as unique entities in their own right, humankind is withholding love and acknowledgement to me. As the saying goes 'As ye sow, so shall ye reap.' Apply this to humankind as a race, and the answer as to what the forthcoming years will hold will become obvious. But for those who are brave enough to stand alone in their recognition of the true Cosmic Love Principle, I and my kind will be there to support them. People have a saying 'God is everywhere', yet they still strive to seek It in some extra-terrestrial domain or obscure heavenly venue. There is a story in your Eastern writings about a man who diligently sought God and, upon finding a most beautiful stone, decided to lift it as God would surely be residing thereunder. However, he became so obsessed with the beauty of the stone that he forgot why he had raised it in the first place. The Infinite Energy you call God is present in all things. Love and respect them and, in so doing, you will love and respect It.

M: Thank you, Mother Sun, for those words of wisdom.

********

Endnotes:
(1) Readers Digest Great Illustrated Dictionary, pp. 1664-1665.
(2) Larousse Encyclopedia of Mythology, pp. 159-160.

Chapter 13

# THE UNIVERSE

For most of us, our concept of the Universe is probably limited to the vast expanse of stellar life we see in our night sky when, in fact, this represents only a minute part of the great Whole. This Universe, we are told, was formed some five thousand million years ago as a result of what has become known as the Big Bang, or point at which some unspecified solid mass, known as a 'singularity', became critical and exploded. However, even the boundaries of orthodoxy are now expanding as new data from more technologically advanced probes rolls in thick and fast. So, although the more orthodox bastions of science still adhere rigidly to the single Universe concept, certain more open minded cosmologists and astrophysicists are daring to suggest that this is but one of many universes, at least one of which may run parallel to our own albeit at a fractionally different frequency.

**Astronomical Data:**
But let us first of all consider what orthodox scientific thinking has to say concerning our Universe. Almost all the matter therein is collected into galaxies, of which there are at least a thousand million in range of our telescopes. The largest of these contains millions of stars. Galaxies are classified according to their shape into normal or barred spirals, which form the vast majority, ellipticals which form 20 per cent, and irregulars which form 5 per cent.

Many of the spiral galaxies are disc-shaped. They have a nucleus of old stars and orbiting arms of young stars. Our own Milky Way is a typical spiral some 100,000 light years across, containing 100,000 million stars. Galaxies form irregular groups, some with thousands of members. The Milky Way is part of a so-called Local Group of about 25, of which the Great Spiral of Andromeda, 2.2 million light years away, is the largest. Our nearest galactic neighbours are the two irregular Magellanic Clouds, 160,000 light years away.

Colliding neutron stars, we are told, mark the end of a pattern of stellar evolution that now appears to be more likely than astronomers once thought. More than half the stars in the sky belong to binary systems; perhaps one in one hundred of the most massive pairs will ultimately become neutron star binaries. Gravitational waves given off by the stars as they orbit each other carry away energy until the stars spiral together and coalesce. These mergers give off radiation that may be detectable from millions of light years away. For those interested in the technical details of the formation of binary neutron stars there is an excellent article, with full illustrations, in *Scientific American*, May 1995, pp. 52-55. However, much as I find the information of considerable interest it is far too technical for a book of this nature. Also, without the illustrations, the words ring hollow.

With all this vast expanse of stellar-life around us, many find themselves questioning why we need to know even more. The answer to this lies, of course, in our limited concept of space-time, which we naturally tend to view from our own perspective. That perspective is, however, limited by the frequency at which both we and our Universe function. There is a space-time coordinate from which this vast collection of galaxies appears no larger than Danuih, and a point in *the speed of time* at which one can move in comfort from *universe to universe*, observing each from those spaces between. I know, because I have visited such a spot and seen it. And there are such areas, about which I hope the genius of the Universe herself will enlighten us.

Over the past decade or so numerous theories have been postulated, some of which border on the metaphysical, while others serve to cast a new light on the nature of energy itself as manifest within our Universe. Likewise, psychiatrists and psychologists have effected parallels between the human mind, quantum theory and universal intelligence. One thing I have learned from all this, however, is that just as we are the minutiae of Gaia (Danuih), she is part of the minutiae of the solar system, the solar system of the galaxy, the galaxy of the Universe, our Universe of the next and so forth. So much for the myth of hominid supremacy. Theoretical physicist Fred Alan Wolf has postulated that the Universe dreams creativity in much the same way that we also create via our dreams. Many of the great discoveries that have changed our lives on this planet originated in the dream state or, should I say, via the right brain accessing the universal databanks. Working on this principle we are all gods in the making but it is only the Timeless Ones who dream the continuity of life into Eternity, the Eternal Dream of continual, infinite creation.

## The Metaphysics:

It has been postulated that the Universe is a giant computer able to access immediately the databanks of everything existing within its boundaries from the tiniest particle to the galactic genii. This being the case, what chance do any of us have of accessing hers? Awareness and knowledge are not synonymous. Knowledge of Gaia, for example, may supply us with the nuts and bolts of her bodily workings but it does not guarantee access to her innermost feelings. Nor does the answer to this lie in the brain, but rather in the field. A cat may possess a brain which, when compared to the hominid organ, is very limited. The cat's field, however, may be another matter altogether. Assuming that feline entity has individuated from the original group soul it has as much access ability as any hominid in a similar stage of development (or similarity of bandwidth).

If all this is starting to sound like gobbledygook may I quote from Dr. Lyall Watson who tells us:

> '... I number theoretical physicists among my friends. They have taught me that the objective world in space and time does not exist and we are forced to deal now not in facts, but in possibilities. Nobody in quantum mechanics talks about impossibilities any more. They have developed a kind of statistical mysticism, and physics becomes very hard to distinguish from metaphysics. And that makes things a little easier for a biologist faced with biological absurdities.
>
> 'Breaking the rules doesn't worry me any more now that I can see that only the principle matters.'[1]

# MY MEETING WITH THE GENIUS
# OF THIS UNIVERSE

As my readers will have no doubt gathered by now I am not writing about these subjects without first experiencing some reality concerning my subject matter. Following the publication of *The Gaia Dialogues* I came upon Dr. John Gribbin's book *In The Beginning* which, as mentioned in earlier chapters, has served to confirm much of what Danuih told me. The back cover of Gribbin's book carries the following statement:

### COULD THE WHOLE UNIVERSE BE ALIVE?

'Ripples in space collected by the COBE (Cosmic Background Explorer) satellite in 1992 clearly confirmed current ideas about the Big Bang. But why do matter and nature's fundamental forces seem specially designed to produce our kind of Universe? Some scientists see the hand of God, others call this a non-question, but Gribbin suggests a deeply satisfying new answer. Going far beyond the Gaia hypothesis, that the Earth is a single living organism, he claims that the galaxies may "operate as supernova nurseries", that one universe can bud from the star-death and "black-hole-bounce" into another, and that such "offspring" are being steadily refined by evolution. In setting out the arguments for these startling conclusions, he has produced one of the most stimulating books of the decade.'

Although the faculty of remote viewing has been available to me since birth, strangely enough my particular gift is more effective when functioning *out of time*. Bearing this in mind I knew there was something I had to do prior to reading Gribbin's chapter on the Universe so that, were I lucky enough to gain some data therefrom, I could substantiate it against Gribbin's vast scientific knowledge. I had been fortunate in my connection with Danuih (Gaia), but was that a one-off? And as for other planetary genii, there is still much to be proven. I decided to step forth and find out.

Having already travelled to a point *outside* our Universe from which the whole scenario appeared no larger than Earth when viewed from the Moon, I returned to these coordinates and, with great timerity, addressed the Universal Genius. 'Is there anyone there who would like to talk to me?' The reply was instantaneous:

'Identify yourself.' This I did and from then on there was no problem. You see, as I have already suggested, she has instant access to all life-forms resident within her boundaries. Besides, as a much time-travelled Time Essence I was well aware of the codes of conduct which exist among such beings. We conversed and she explained many things to me, not the least of which was that she, too, had her limitations. But why do I refer to her as a 'she', when, to me, she was simply a field of energy? I put it to her this way: 'one of my particles is at present trapped in a hominid body on the planet we call Earth' (which she knew, anyway), 'and, as you know, it is always a help to the hominid brain if it can visualize a force-field in some form which it deems to be approachable'. She understood me immediately. 'How will this do?' The vision she made for me was of a feminine figure which vaguely resembled a hominid form but not of this planet. It was tall and clothed in pale green. The eyes were wide but highly slanted, and the hair long, copious, and bright red. I knew then for sure that I was dealing with a life-form which had started its evolutionary cycle as a fire elemental. She read my thoughts. 'You have wondered why my Universe is black – it is because it is actually a black hole – a place for refining all that passes through it into other universes.' And there was much, much more. However, before this chapter is completed I am hoping that she will allow me to engage in a dialogue with her which could, perhaps, serve to explain some of the anomalies which still face science today.

So, how does this experience, plus the information given, stand up in the light of current scientific knowledge? Let us take it a step at a time. Why 'feminine'? Surely this is simply my brain's interpretation of the negative/receptive aspect of an electrical field. In other words, in the chain of universes they must run from positive to negative? The answer to this could possibly lie in a paper by Edward Tryon of the City University of New York, published in 1973, which Gribbin cites, in which the author suggested that our entire Universe might simply be a fluctuation of the vacuum. Gribbin comments:

> 'The point Tryon jumped off from – the secret of making universes out of nothing at all, as vacuum fluctuations – is that the gravitational energy of the Universe is negative.'[2]

As for our Universe being a black hole, Gribbin's book is packed with the evidence for this. Here are a couple of examples:

'We actually live inside a huge black hole − a black hole so big that it contains millions of other black holes inside itself. And what is more, we have a pretty good idea of what happens to anything that collapses towards a singularity inside a black hole

'... the realization that our own Universe seems to have been born out of a singularity, and the evidence confirmed by C O B E, that we live inside a black hole, pulls the rug from under the argument that we need not concern ourselves with what goes on inside a black hole. We certainly do want to know what goes on inside our Universe!

'The idea of the Universe as a black hole is not new, although until recently it was distinctly unfashionable. As far as I know, I was the first person to describe the Universe in these words, in an unsigned editorial commentary in the journal *Nature* in 1971 (volume 232, page 440). Scarcely anybody took the notion seriously, because nobody then realized that the Universe is dominated gravitationally by dark matter. But today, scarcely anybody doubts this picture. And if all the complexity of galaxies, stars, planets and organic life has emerged from the singularity in which our Universe was born, within a black hole, could not something similar be happening at the hearts of other black holes?'[3]

As to the concept of the Universe being, like Gaia, a living entity, Gribbin continues:

'In his published papers even Smolin has stopped short of suggesting that the Universe is alive. But heredity is an essential feature of life, and this description of the evolution of universes works only if we are dealing with living systems. I believe that our Universe − like all universes − is literally alive. In this picture, universes pass on their characteristics to their offspring with only minor changes, just as people pass on their characteristics to their children with only minor changes.'[4]

Bingo! And there is much, much more, all of which has served to restore my confidence in knowledge gained from my conversations with non-hominid intelligences encountered during my journeys through time. The new mathematical concept of space-time, Gribbin tells us, is represented by a set of four dimensions (three of space and one of time) just like our own, but with *all* the dimensions at right angles to *all* the familiar dimensions of our own spacetime.[5] And then we have those 'virtual particles', which we can't see, but which are said to be produced by quantum fluctuations in the vacuum. The easiest of these to identify are the particles of light, photons, which have zero mass, which probably gave birth to the 'photon belt' scare which many New Age adherents fell for in 1992.

According to certain dubious reports, and scientifically unsubstantiated channelled information, our solar system is supposedly destined to enter a photon belt before the end of this century. The effect of such a radiation belt on Earth would be an excitation of atoms (?) resulting in all things becoming luminescent. The solar system would take some 2000 years to pass through this belt during which time another Ice Age would occur. All electrical systems would be affected but photon power would be developed in lieu. Scientists contacted at the time by *Omega New Age Directory* stated that they knew of no such phenomenon and, if there really were such a thing, its light would be recognized and analyzed well in advance. Needless to say, on the date originally given for this occurrence nothing happened; – yet another instance of the folly of believing messages from so-termed 'higher sources' without first checking the real facts. At the time several people asked me if there was anything in it. I told them 'no', but, rather than take my word, I advised them to ring the Greenwich Observatory, whose astronomers would soon put them right.

Gribbin suggests that there are actually 'virtual universes', the implication being that these could either exist side-by-side with our own Universe or 'simultaneously within'; parallel, perhaps. Which reminds me of my old Paschat teaching that, within what we can only conceive of as 'infinity', there are an infinite number of permutations of experiences being undergone *simultaneously*. For example, we may, in our present life, be injured in a train crash, whereas in another, virtual universe that crash might never have occurred and our lives would have proceeded in a different fashion. Likewise with wars and other major events. What would many of us be doing now had WW2 not taken place? The ability to access such 'virtual' dimensions might provide us with the answer to much of life's seeming unfairness and, perhaps, explain how the evening-up process actually takes place within the realms of ultimate timelessness.

There is so much wonderful information in Gribbin's book, which he presents with a scholarship I could not hope to match, that I have no hesitation in recommending it to anyone sufficiently open minded and interested in the true process of creation, rather than the claptrap we are served up with from those religious sources so succinctly described by Danuih as 'chess pieces in the hominid ego game'. (See *The Gaia Dialogues*.)

From my point of view there are also many, many questions I would like to ask of the Universal Genius, both for myself and on behalf of others. For example, what was the nature of the region I was occupying during my viewing of the body of the Universe while communicating with my field? And how do the archetypes fit in with all this? Perhaps the time has come to hand over to her — if she is willing — for these, and many other answers. Incidentally, during our first meeting I asked her if she could give me a name by which I might address her. She explained, of course, that names are simply sounds which resonate to the frequency of the field. The sound left over from the Big Bang may still be heard at the long/microwave end of the electromagnetic spectrum (the interference we hear on our radios when they are not correctly tuned). She suggested something with sshh. I came out with Shâna (pronounced Shayner. 'Since you must have a sonic by which to recognize me, that's as good as anything,' she replied. So Shâna she became to me. And now for the 'handover'.

## The Dialogue:

S: Since the arrangement for this dialogue has already been agreed between us I will proceed with your earlier-voiced questions. There are 'spaces' between universes and it was from just such a point in space-time that you viewed my body. However, since nature abhors a vacuum such spaces are well and truly occupied by non-physical entities you might refer to as 'archetypes'. Each physical cosmic structure, be it a planet or a universe, is influenced by different archetypes which vary according to the needs of the genotypes concerned. Such intelligences are of a unique evolutionary stream, having a close affinity with the Timeless Ones by whom they are directly 'employed'. Their task is to emphasize and stimulate the growth of the principles they represent as appropriate to the evolving consciousness with which they are specifically dealing. The archetypal energies involved in the Danuih experience are, for example, different from those which were concerned with Paschat growth and evolvement. The archetypes are not planetary genii, nor are they gods in the accepted polytheistic understanding of this term, although such Beings may well reflect their energies as required by those under their specific influence, in their care or under their instruction. I hope that answers you.

M: Some scientists seem to have more paraphysical knowledge than many so-termed 'mystics' and metaphysicists. Why is this?

S: Because they brought the knowledge with them. In other words, they are simply accessing their own databanks for information they already learned in mine or other Universes. Of course they may not be prepared to admit this which is, in fact, a good thing as they would lose credibility were they to speak as you do regarding what you knew before you were born into the body via which you now approach me. Being aware of possible prejudicial attitudes prevalent in their time, the cautionary mode was programmed in prior to their birth.

M: That makes sense. Now may I ask you about the super-string process and at which point separations are effected into the many different evolutionary streams on, say, the body of Danuih, so that they end up as a man, a cat, a tree, a fire elemental, etc.?

S: The actual point of separation varies with each species so I cannot give you exact data. Besides, even if I were to it would not be understood at present, most scientists being more concerned with the nuts and bolts of physics rather than the psychology of the developing personality which is born from the group-experience undergone during the early days of the evolutionary process. Your Dr. Gribbin is, of course, correct in allying evolution with cosmology. In fact, everything in my body which you refer to as your Universe goes through the same growth procedures. Group entities emerge from the primaeval soup concocted by early particle/wave formations, which slowly separate into streams, the nature of which vary according to conditions offered by the fostering entity, in your present case, Danuih. As these group entities evolve, discrete particle/wave packets start to individuate therefrom. All living things, from the minutest particle to the greatest imaginable mass, have a consciousness or field although, during their cosmic youth, they lack 'awareness'. This is something that only comes with experience and understanding. In other words, increase in awareness is the deciding factor in the expansion of the field. The more aware, and therefore wiser a field becomes, the more it is able to connect with other aware fields and exchange information, thus adding to the databanks of all concerned. No species is therefore superior to another since all eventually reunite at a given point in Timelessness. Hence the folly of separatism, speciesism and cosmic racism. I am given to understand that this ultimate fusion of fields takes place in the region of the Timeless Ones, but since I have not yet attained to that exalted position I can only go on intuition and cosmic heresay.

M: Can you tell us more about those entities whom you and Vulcan refer to as the 'Timeless Ones' and Danuih calls the 'Time Lords', and where do their 'progeny' fit into the picture?

S: Those destined for the Time Path are born, not made. Let us return to our primaeval soup theory. Among the divers life forms emerging therefrom is one particular stream, the individual aspects of which are destined for the Time Path. This stream represents the fifth element, the other four being Fire, Air, Water and Earth. Following their individuation process, and during the course of their 'studies', such entities may be required to travel through many universes wherein it becomes necessary for them to sample life within the confines of different evolutionary forms. This does not mean that they necessarily belong to those streams into which they occasionally incarnate, but rather that they need the experience as part of the agenda set for them. Time Essences always travel light, seldom accumulating the debris of material possessions *en route*. And, since they endeavour to avoid extremes, they are unlikely to be found in either the mansions of the rich or the hovels of the poor. They are by nature hard workers; they have to be in order to survive the ordeals which they are required to face. However, I am given to understand that, in spite of the difficulties such beings encounter, they are also blessed with the necessary energies to overcome them and survive. Danuih's Time Lord concept differs slightly from mine in that, from my point of vision, there are grades within that structure. At the apex, however, all time and all creation merges into the ONE, and yet that ONE is composed of the many who have attained to that Ultimate, Infinite state: my aforementioned fusion of souls! There are, however, Time Beings below that point who, with the help of their elemental brethren, orchestrate the creation of universes, and it would be these Beings with whom Danuih would be more familiar. With all due respect to Danuih, may I dispense with the 'progeny' tag and fill you in a little more on the actual nature of these Time Essences. During your scientists' search for a unifying factor which would combine with the four known energy sources of the cosmos – the weak and strong nuclear forces, electromagnetism and gravity – to create a 'Theory of Everything' (TOE) various ideas have emerged. Now may I give you my version of the picture. The four accepted energy sources relate to what metaphysicists refer to as The Primary Four: the weak nuclear force to Water, the strong to Fire, electromagnetism to Air and gravity to Earth. The fifth force for which they seek is, of course, Time. However, at the primary particle level, the young Time Essences are bound by the Group Soul from which they eventually individuate in much the same way as elementals who have gained their fourfold natures. Time Essences, incidentally, are more closely akin to Fire than to the other three elements. You may call the young ones neutrinos or whatever name you wish, their early behaviour patterns according with present scientific knowledge of such particles. In fact a Time Essence could, as in your own case, also experience as a fire elemental or a Paschat. But as you well know you started as neither, whereas I entered into primary existence as the former. I feel I should make it clear to your readers that for those who travel that particular Path the journey is no picnic. It is a long and painful one and its travellers are not to be envied. They may make friends along the roads of experience but they also attract enmities, especially among Danuih's errant brood who are inclined to persecute anything they feel to be in some way 'different' from themselves. But then your readers do not need me to tell them this, it is in their history books for all to read. A final comment on this subject: I have often heard the question voiced as to why those mythological characters who are credited with the ability to pass through the dark regions unharmed are inevitably portrayed in animal form, the Egyptian Anubis and the Atlantean Akhantuih being prime examples. Well, as far as your planet is concerned, it is among the animals that the strongest and most reliable fields (souls) are to be found, fields pure enough in essence to be suitable companions to accompany the Time Essences during their ceaseless travels.

M: Thank you Shâna. And now I must ask you the inevitable: – your view on the subject of God?

S: The singular God idea which Danuih's hominids have manufactured among themselves in order to fulfil an emotional need is alien to me. Many humans have become obsessed with this concept to their detriment, their theology preventing them from opening their minds to the real truth. Also, as your planetary friends have explained to you, Earth hominids are taken up with their own importance to the extent that even their favoured deity is viewed by them as being in their own image and likeness. This is a cosmically immature stance from which they need to free themselves before they can cope with real cosmic knowledge.

M: People have asked me if you can access their databanks, which naturally brings me round to the question of your size as relative to our own.

S: Size is relative to the angle and space occupied by the viewer. In the faster frequencies of inter-time I may be seen as comparatively small, since time, at a given frequency, has a telescopic effect. I put it to you this way: how many hominids are able to access the databanks of the minute bacteria that live in their gut? And yet I am expected to be in tune with everything that exists within my body. I hear your mystics saying 'the Universe will provide'. Of course I do not sit at a table deciding whether this or that being occupying my vast domains is worthy of the assistance for which they ask. One could say I delegate. But what really happens is that everything finds its own level *which accords with the level at which the request is made.* People may think they have a hot line to God, as they call it, whereas, in fact, there is really no such thing. What happens in many 'mystical' experiences is that the brain obligingly provides what its software has taught the suppliant to believe. An excellent example of this is the stigmata phenomena so beloved of certain religions. Historians have been well aware for a long time that the Romans did not insert the nails of crucifixion at the points at which the stigmata bleeding often takes place. But, since the software has suggested differently, the nervous system acts out the appropriate commands.

M: Could you please comment on 'dark matter'?

S: There is little I can add to what is already known. The bulk of my body is made up of the stuff. The bits and pieces visible to you are simply the trimmings on the cake, if you like. However, I am pleased to read (through your eyes) of the discovery that (some?) neutrinos do have a mass after all, albeit a small one, which information is calculated to open yet more doors of cosmic knowledge along the lines I referred to earlier.

M: There are those who are bound to ask me whether they can access your databanks.

S: If they are able to identify themselves cosmically, providing their field is of a sufficient bandwidth capable of sustaining the kind of electrical charge (radiation) I emit, then yes. However, should they attempt to do so without the necessary 'safety equipment' they would blow more than a few fuses. In other words they would be liable to receive a severe shock, both physical and mental. It should also be borne in mind that intelligence has nothing to do with all this; the brain accommodates the needs of the genotype only and should not be taken as an indication of the bandwidth of the field. Two of your cats have access to my databanks but, unlike yourself, they do not have the cerebral software essential to the expression of their perceptions. There is, however, an unwritten law which operates throughout all universes, which designates a form of *carte blanche* access to Time Essences of all ages, throughout all regions, regardless of their inclination or evolutionary status. Many may resent having to grant this access, or may even attempt to bar it, but they are eventually obliged to submit and make their databanks available on demand. Since, therefore, we have no option, it is always advisable to be polite and accommodating. In terms of physics, a neutrino is going to pass through the body of Danuih (or any other mass for that matter) whether she likes it or not, so perhaps it behoves her, or any of us, both to accept the situation and benefit by learning from it.

M: Are all black hole universes fiery and passive/receptive?

S: Generally, yes, because they are in the process of gestation. Please consider also the idea that not all universes are black holes, some being electromagnetically positive/active. Passing positively charged universes seed negative/receptive universes. (I fear your lack of appropriate scientific terms is proving a hindrance to me here.) There are more universes than your scientists could dream of at present, each with its own quality and unique evolutionary program, but the knowledge will slowly unfold to the extent that the esoterica of your todays will become the accepted exoterica of your tomorrows. The cycle of universal existence could be seen as a macrocosm of your own in that within my body there is a constant replacement of cells; planets, suns, etc. are born and die in cycles. And, just as your bodies have their major organs which are orchestrated cerebrally in concert with their genetic program, so I have mine. Likewise my orderly growth will eventually succumb to the chaos of old age. It is truly a matter of 'as above, so below'.

M: Do you really dream creation as Wolf suggests?

S:  I dream, but only in respect of the events taking place within my own body which you refer to as the Universe. We all create within our dreams but those dreams are, in turn, limited by our bandwidth. Only The Timeless Ones know all and therefore dream all; and it is only at the apex of Timelessness, the Great Infinity, that the dream becomes the instant reality.

M:  Thank you, Shâna. I shall have to stop there. I hope we will be able to talk again.

S:  Of course, but not for public consumption. That episode in your life is, as you already know, about to close. But I hope you will always count me among your friends.

M:  Rest assured of that, dear Shâna.

Endnotes:
(1) Watson, L. *Gifts of Unknown Things*, pp. 146-147.
(2) Gribbin, J. *In the Beginning: The Birth of the Living Universe*, p. 248.
(3) *Ibid*, p. 243.
(4) *Ibid*, p. 252.
(5) *Ibid*, p. 244.

# SUMMARY

## COMMENT

I feel I must preface this final chapter by emphasizing the fact that being a Time Essence does not designate me as superior to any other life form. While using a hominid body I am naturally subject to the limitations of both the brain and the software, which frequently precludes me from expressing many 'truths' in terms appropriate to the present day hominid scenario, the margin of error tending to vary with the subject matter. Readers are therefore advised not to take any of what is written as 'gospel' but to make up their own minds (which they will do anyway), accepting or rejecting according to their own personal stages of spiritual growth or awareness.

Fitting the numerous inquiries into the limited space allotted by this book has proved difficult to say the least. There are still many, many questions I and my friends would like to put to Shâna. For example, in *The Mind of God*, Paul Davies speculates as to the possibility of the Universe being self-creative which would do away with the need for a 'creator' in the popularly accepted form of the Christian god. Davies also considers many other theories such as the Universe as a self-programming computer. The theists' reply to this one is naturally that all computers rely on a programmer which brings us round full circle to the idea that this function is naturally carried out by a supreme deity: God. But surely what we are faced with here is humankind's need for a peg upon which to hang everything or a convenient pigeon-hole which makes the tidying-up process so much easier. Davies explores real worlds as against their 'virtual' possibilities.

Time, and the role played by its energy, is constantly rearing its head in the many dissertations now in print on the subject of the birth, *raison d'être* and eventual demise of the Universe with which we are all familiar. In fact, Time is so intrinsically bound up with the whole process of creation that one wonders how its true position as the elusive 'fifth force' has not yet been officially acknowledged. In his pursuit of the creative quest Davies offers the following quote which I feel to be completely appropriate to the Time factor:

Time and Eternity: The Fundamental Paradox of Existence

> Eternity is time
> Time, eternity
> To see the two as opposites
> Is Man's perversity.
>
> *The Book of Angelus Silesius*[1]

Shâna tells me that her program issued from the Timeless Ones, beings of pure, unmanifest energy who exist in a dimension so exalted that even she cannot fully comprehend their true nature; and even within that structure, if one could call it such, there are levels of awareness ranging from the creators of universes like her own soma to the apex, or point from which all consciousness originated and to which it is inevitably destined to return, albeit wiser for the experience and awareness gained during its evolutionary sojourn. So, you may argue, why not simplify matters by calling that point 'God'? Because, as Shâna has pointed out, it is not a single cell as such, but an infinite point of fully aware *collective* consciousness. My impression is that she is by no means denying the existence of a Supreme Creative Force but rather denigrating humankind's limiting concept of it as a singular Mind/Being *in its own image and likeness.*

Those readers who require rational answers to the mysteries of virtual existence should read *The Mind of God.* On the other hand, there may be many among you who would prefer to hear it straight from the horse's mouth, as seen, felt and experienced by the Universe herself and those few celestial bodies within our solar system whose energies would appear to exert such a powerful influence on our lives; in which case *Cosmic Connections* is the book for you.

# DANGER ZONES

Of all the dialogues listed in this book I have found Shâna's the most stimulating. However, the acquisition of such knowledge has not been without its pain, frustration and physical side-effects. The central and autonomic nervous systems naturally react when subjected to unfamiliar frequencies although, once accustomed to these, they soon settle down. Likewise the immune system which can, in f act, become stronger and more effective if allowed to cope on its own, especially with the numerous and varied types of energies I have been dealing with during the writing of this book.

Many people are already asking me how these communications have affected me. The experience overall has been both exhilarating and disturbing. Having once opened these doors, however, I cannot close them; but I can at least control the locking systems. As for those who may aspire to tread such dangerous grounds, a few timely words of warning: I am a Time-Essence and as such I carry the necessary identification disk. But, the pitfalls being too numerous to cite, my advice to would-be experimenters is: don't! Stay with the theory by all means but forgo the practical until you are absolutely secure in your cosmic identity and thoroughly familiar with the highways of Time. Agreed we all have to start somewhere, but our destined paths may point in different directions and to stray from those paths without the necessary 'maps' can result in becoming lost in time.

There are many matters I have discussed with Shâna and the planetary, solar and stellar genii which, being concerned with the individual fields themselves, are private and not for publication. However, I would like to offer a few observations, especially in relation to my dialogues with Shâna. I was particularly interested in her comments regarding animals here on Earth since, according to certain (obviously erroneous) Eastern teachings, animals are a lower form of life than hominids. Nowhere else among my many cosmic contacts have I ever encountered this belief, all my other sources agreeing with the 'separate stream' doctrine explained so clearly by Shâna in the last Chapter; while all the celestial genii were unanimous in their condemnation of humankind's attitude towards other life forms on Earth.

As many students of esoterica will be aware, most mythological cycles feature a character to whom some superior force has granted the right of safe passage through time and space: the ability to negotiate the 'dark regions' (black holes?) without fear of danger or destruction therein. To the ancient Egyptians it was Anubis the 'Opener of the Ways', portrayed as a dark jackal or hunting dog, to whom this privilege was accorded, while the Atlanteans favoured Akhantuih, the black panther who could pass through the chaotic worlds in complete safety; and there are endless other examples. Perhaps, as Shâna has hinted, the Time Essences take their companion animals with them on their exploratory journeys, or maybe they even assume that animal form themselves (shape-shift) during such travels. Either way, the animals come out on top.

However, as Shâna has explained, these tales are not meant to convey the idea that such journeys through the extremities of chaos and order are without their stress, any more than the fact that one has emerged from a traumatic experience guarantees that one has come through unscathed. In the final analysis all of us – be we animals, plants, elements, planetary genii or whatever – are engaged in the great journey of discovery that is evolution. The paths we take may well be different but, since all roads eventually lead to the centre, both the joys and sorrows we experience during these journeys serve to add to the infinite data-banks of Eternity.


## THE FOUR FORCES (PLUS TIME)

Shâna's information concerning the relationship between the four acknowledged energy 'forces' and the four elements, plus a fifth element (Time) which corresponds with the scientifically speculated reconciling factor, or 'fifth force', makes both scientific and metaphysical sense. Let us start with the known facts.

*The Gravitational Force* is universal in that every particle feels the force of gravity according to its mass or energy. Gravity, Hawking tells us, is the weakest of the four forces in that we would not notice it were it not for the fact that it can act over large distances and is always attractive. But is it not the interplay between Time and gravity which effects the ageing process?

*The Electromagnetic Force* is much stronger than gravity. It carries both positive and negative charges which react differently towards each other in that the force between two positive charges is repulsive as is the force between two negative charges, whereas a positive charge is attractive to a negative charge. It is the electromagnetic attraction between negatively charged electrons and positively charged protons in the nucleus that causes the electrons to orbit the nucleus of an atom, just as gravitational attraction causes the Earth to orbit the Sun.

*The Weak Nuclear Force* is responsible for radioactivity which acts on all matter particles of spin 1/2, but not on particles of spin 0, 1 or 2 such as photons and gravitons. One interesting factor that research has highlighted in relation to this force is that what appear to be a number of completely different particles at low energies are in fact found to be the same type of particle, only in different states. *At high energies all these particles behave similarly.* Very metaphysical, no?

*The Strong Nuclear Force* holds the quarks together in the proton and neutron and holds the protons and neutrons together in the nucleus of an atom., In other words, it is a *binding force*.

Time, we are told, did not exist before the Big Bang, which

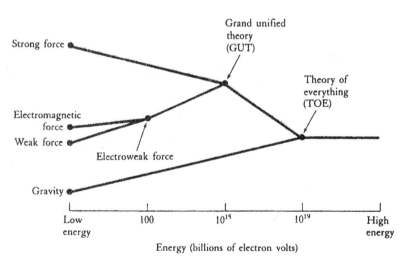

Energy (billions of electron volts)

Enormous energies are required to unify the four forces of nature. It is thought the four forces were once unified at the higher energies characteristic of the universe soon after the big bang, and indeed a theory that unifies the weak force and the electromagnetic force has already been verified for energies of a few hundred GeV.

makes metaphysical sense since, according to Shâna, universes are created by the Timeless Ones who imbue them with their energies – the fifth Force – without which we would not exist, *the manifestation of matter being contingent upon the slowing down of the speed of time.*

After delving deeper into both the scientific and mythological implications of the above, the correlation between myth and fact became increasingly obvious, thus adding weight to the idea that the originators of many of the myths were technologically advanced scientists who found themselves faced with the onerous task of encoding their scientific knowledge in such a way that it would be ultimately recognized in years to come. Taking into account religious/social/metaphysical developments destined to take place over the ensuing centuries, they decided that the best way would be to personalize those cosmic forces with which they were familiar, so that their *essence*, if not the actual knowledge of their true nature within the scientific context, would be perpetuated in the religion, and, eventually the psychology of future generations. Bearing this in mind, and, being heedful of my own limitations in these interpretations, here are a few preliminary connections I have been able to effect:

The **STRONG FORCE** is *orderly*
(as represented by the archetypes of Stability)

The **WEAK FORCE** is *chaotic*
(as represented by the archetypes of Subtle Change)

**ELECTROMAGNETISM** is *chaotic*
(as represented by the archetypes of Physical Change)

**GRAVITY** is *orderly*
(as represented by the archetypes of Solidity)
**TIME** contains elements of both *order and chaos*
(as represented by specialized archetypes).

**TIME** *contains elements*
of both *order* and *chaos* as represented
by specialized archetypes

## ARCHETYPAL ASSOCIATIONS

*Strong Force* energies are exemplified in such mythological characters as Hephaestus, Vulcan, Wayland, and similarly natured 'smithy' deities, all of whom were associated with the binding force, or *conversion of energy into matter.* Likewise the deities of wisdom, philosophy, science, architecture and masonry such as the Egyptian Ptah and the Atlantean Philaeia. It is also interesting to observe that in the ancient Egyptian reference to the *khet-khet* or double fire – the Fire of Solidification and the Fire of Dispersion – the energies of Isis were associated with the former and those of Nephthys with the latter, which would seem to place Isis in this category and her sister Nephthys in the next.

*Weak Force* energies are expressed via those watery divinities associated with dissemination/dispersion: Dionysus, Osiris, Neptune/Poseidon, Nephthys, Mananan etc., and those lunar energies, the diffusive/fragmentatory qualities of which are well known metaphysically (and also encountered in the fields of medicine and psychology!). One is reminded of the radioisotope strontium 90, used in high-energy beta-emissions in certain nuclear power sources, and constituting a radiation hazard in fall-out.

*Electromagnetism* accommodates the expression of those dual-natured, disruptive energies which function via the medium of communication, movement (motion) and change: Set, Loki, Lucifer, Kali, Morrigan, Sekhmet, the Atlantean Khiet-Sîn and Jung's 'Mercurius' being examples. It should be born in mind, however, that chaotic energies are just as essential to progress/evolution as those of an orderly nature. Sekhmet, for example, was known to the ancient Egyptians as 'the enemy of chaos'; in other words she, like the genius of the planet Uranus (see Chapter 6), represents the phase transition, or point at which chaos turns to order, which inevitably serves to highlight any imperfections.

*Gravity* is represented by those divinities emphasizing the archetypes of Order: – Horus, Zeus, Baldur, Hathor, Dana, Bran, the Atlantean Danuih etc., also both the male and female solar deities, without whose gravitational pull our planet would not stay in orbit (note Hawking's earlier reference in Endnote 2), although the solar role in the chain of the conversion of energy to matter could also relate them to the Strong nuclear force. However, Zeus' supplanting of Cronus (Time) – destiny decreeing his own inevitable dethronement at some future date – (see Chapter 9), Set appropriating the throne of Osiris, and similar mythological take-overs serve to exemplify the phase transition from Order to Chaos resulting in the inevitable disintegration of organized systems.

*Time.* Over the aeons, several divinities have emerged who have acted as *reflectors* for the energies of the Time archetypes: Cronus, Hermes, Merlin, Thoth, Sîn, Aion. These were often portrayed in the judicial role, or as testers, Thoth, for example, being the judge in the recurring combat between Horus (Order) and Set (Chaos). However, in view of what Shâna has told us, the true Time Essences are represented by those mythological characters who have been granted *carte blanche* safety through all realms, both of light and darkness; the Egyptian Anubis, the Atlantean Akhantuih, Merlin's black dog, etc. whom the ancients, being all too aware of hominid limitations and frailties, wisely portrayed in animal form. Those who, during their endless journeys through countless universes, gather *information* which they duly pass on at their next cosmic port of call.

Those sources of pure, unmanifest energy, which I have elected to refer to as the Archetypes, and who, Shâna tells us, work in concert with the Timeless Ones, are the 'minds' or consciousness behind all these principles. Dare we, perhaps, borrow a page from Dr. Greenfield's book (see Chapter 1) and liken them to the crew of the Starship *Universe*; think about it!

For those interested in effecting a correlation at the primary particle level, an in-depth study of quantum theory will serve to highlight which particles (elementals) are connected with which FORCE. For example, not all particles interconnect with others, while there is also the question of stability. Time particles, on the other hand, interact with *all* Four Forces. In my book *Time: The Ultimate Energy*[3] I have touched on primary particle preliminaries, but for those requiring more specific facts the Lederman and Schramm work supplies a mine of up-to-date information.

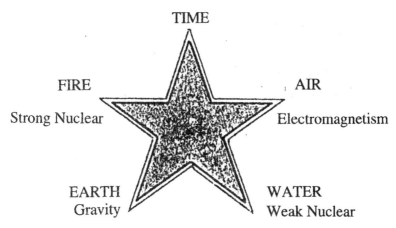

*The Four Forces with their elemental associations*

According to Einstein's theories of Special and General Relativity, mass and energy are inter changeable. I therefore propose that the speed of Time at any given point on its scale (which is yet to be scientifically acknowledged and established) is relative to the density of the mass - matter being *time slowed down*. Thus the energy of Time is essential to the manifestation of mass and likewise its reconversion to energy. As Professor Stewart pointed out to me, the slowing down of time in relation to that which is observable may be evidenced in the spectrum of electromagnetic radiation, the frequency/kHz (indicating the cycles per second), showing the process quite clearly (see p 190).

Interestingly enough, the following quote from Lederman and Schramm brings us back full circle to what Shâna has told us:

> 'The line of reasoning guiding modern theoretical physics can be expressed as "Underneath it all, isn't there just *one* force that produces all particles and their interactions?" '[4]

For my part I am happy to bid science adieu at this point as I will inevitably be criticized by both metaphysical fundamentalists and scientific purists either for getting too technical on the one hand or failing to effect sufficient substantiation on the other. Besides, my job as I see it is to start the ball rolling in this direction, so it will be up to those wiser, or more erudite, to take it from here.

# Spectrum of Electromagnetic Radiation

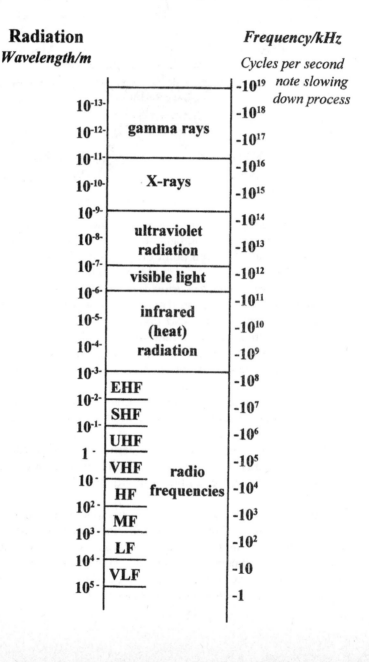

## THE CREATIVE DREAM

The existence of virtual worlds parallel to our 'real' world has become a popular subject for debate among theoretical physicists, theologians and psychologists to the extent that it is no longer a no-man's-land inhabited only by the lunatic fringe. For example, the dividing line between what we perceive as reality and the parallel world of dreams is so fine as to be indistinct. Through dreams we explore the many options of experience relative to our stance in time, such 'virtual' scenarios serving to complement (or compensate for?) the 'actual' occurrences in our daily lives. Every living thing from the minutest particle to the greatest imaginable mass has both its virtual and actual realities, and that goes for the wave (field) as well. The term 'dream' could, therefore, be seen as covering many contingencies such as the aforementioned creative impulse accredited to the Timeless Ones, or some other supreme deity according to one's beliefs or inclinations.

As far as humankind is concerned, however, sleep is an essential ingredient to the balance between soma/psyche/field which guarantees good mental and physical health. Not the unnatural sleep of sedatives but real sleep, which scientists now know to be a complex alternation of at least five different stages. Via dreams we negotiate the worlds of NDEs (near-death-experiences), OOBs (out of the body experiences) and similar paraphysical phenomena, that inevitable 'dark tunnel' so vividly described by those who have seen it representing a mini-wormhole (black-hole?) between the particle and its fuzzy wave world of non-locality. It has also been speculated that our dreams contain the seeds of future reality; we dream the future, or does the dream 'create' the scenario which is eventually replayed at the actual level? Food for thought, indeed. I could cite numerous case histories to support the latter but this book is aimed to deal specifically with other aspects of life at given levels only.

Animals also dream, cats in particular, since they spend much of their time asleep. Coincidental? Hardly. Scientists have now discovered that their brains contain a substance which tells them when to go to sleep, and that same compound may likewise control sleep in humans. Cats, however, unlike humans, don't suffer from insomnia but, perhaps, at some future date when scientists have enough information to effect a synthesization, many an insomniac may have good reason to bless these dear creatures. Or must we wait until we are eventually relieved of the intolerable stresses of modern-day living to the extent that we can, like the cats, rebalance our own sleep-inducing chemicals?

It is interesting to observe how information appropriate to the period in question is inevitably released in what may appear to the rational minded to be perfectly natural ways, a classic example being the recent discovery of a parallel solar system in the constellation of Pegasus and its sun, a star called 51 Peg, 40 light years away. (*See illustration opposite.*)

Can it be sheer coincidence that Pegasus, a constellation in the northern hemisphere, adjoins Aquarius? Doubtless the same principle can also be applied to nanotechnology: atomic-scale engineering capable of remaking the world atom by atom, in any form we fancy (or so we are told!) while time travel – once confined to the realms of sci-fi – has now received the stamp of approval from no less than that doyen of cosmologists and theoretical physicists, Professor Stephen Hawking himself! The mind boggles! However, let us take our leave of such futuristic scenarios and return to the here and now.


## GENETIC MEMORY OR 'FIELD' DATA-BANKS?

I wonder how many people realize that, in supposedly accessing their former 'lives', they are actually effecting genetic rather than field (spiritual) data? I have often been approached by people claiming to have 'been with me' in various relationships or situations which have supposedly occurred in certain periods during Danuih's vast history, none of which, I fear, are true. What they are probably accessing are, however, the data-banks of the *genes of the body I am currently wearing*. I learned this myself the hard way by discovering, in one particular instance, that I was not dealing with a former 'life' as such, but the experiences undergone by a genetic ancestor, although in essence I was never that person. I also find myself emotionally affected by ancestral events when I read about them in history, but this is the genes talking, not the field. So, beware the genetic trap and try not to confuse it with the field reincarnatory factor. However, it is possible for the field (psyche) to be attracted to a particular genetic strain, thus effecting a synchronization between the two systems. This would result in a dual emphasis of concentrated energy focussed on the historical period involved and its relative ethos. An energy input of this nature would tend to produce a personality who is destined to leave his or her mark on world history.

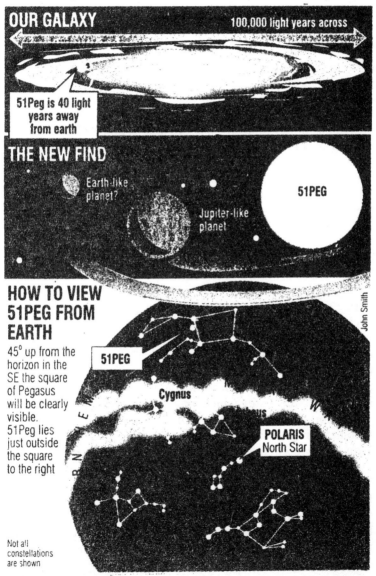

**OUR GALAXY**     100,000 light years across

51Peg is 40 light years away from earth

**THE NEW FIND**

Earth-like planet?

Jupiter-like planet

51PEG

**HOW TO VIEW 51PEG FROM EARTH**

45° up from the horizon in the SE the square of Pegasus will be clearly visible.
51Peg lies just outside the square to the right

51PEG

Cygnus

POLARIS
North Star

John Smith

Not all constellations are shown

## OUT OF THE CLOSET

This book has constituted something of a watershed for me. Ever since childhood I have been aware of my true identity and my role in Time, but fear – of appearing different, of attracting ridicule, of being seen as a suitable candidate for the people in white coats – has demanded that I restrict my knowledge to the limitations of esoteric 'orthodoxy'. In other words, I have been obliged to pay lip service to the accepted interpretations of metaphysical teachings while all the time being aware of many of their origins and true meanings. Science has, in a sense, become my liberator in that it has supplied me with more acceptable terms of reference and yet, because I have no qualifications within any of its disciplines, I am still the outsider, existing in a kind of paraphysical 'no-man's-land'. However, having already poked my head out of the proverbial closet in *The Gaia Dialogues*, complete vacation of said 'cubicle' now seems appropriate. Besides, the target needs to be moved before the commencement of the brickbat hurling that this book will obviously evoke.

## THE OBSERVATIONS AND CONFESSIONS OF A TIME ESSENCE

Before embarking on a description of my personal identity I need to clarify a few important points. I am neither a 'Master', 'Adept', or any other such exalted personality, such icons having no reality outside of the hominid collective, which unconsciously created them as criteria against which to measure individual stages of development. My 'field', or spirit if you prefer, is a single aspect of a five-fold Time Entity which experiences alternating periods of separation from the matrix (chaos) followed by periods of reunification therewith (order). I and the other four Essences which form our group were first brought to this planet by our 'Father' in the long, long, prehistoric past, our separation, or five-fold individuation from the matrix (which was essential for the negotiation of hominid bodies) representing a period of chaos for us which was to last for thousands of Earth years. In future times, when humanity has learned to appreciate the true nature of Time, people will come to understand more about our 'kind' and the nature of our commitment.

Since our first exposure to Earth conditions *each of us has incarnated once only* for a specific purpose, or mission. (Before I am questioned regarding the term 'Father' may I hasten to add that this is purely arbitrary, the Being in question being spiritually androgynous.) Therefore, knowing the hominid predisposition towards 'identity discs', if I am to be 'labelled', perhaps the Fool in the Tarot would be more appropriate. Like him, I am the Eternal Time Traveller who, accompanied by my faithful companion (feline in my case), is ever ready to rush headlong into the uncharted territories of the great Unknown. This was explained to me in a 'dream' experience some years ago when I saw Eternity stretched forth before me while a presence, whom I recognized as my Father, stood behind me urging me to step forward. 'Keep walking,' he said, 'and I shall always be walking behind you.' But there was nothing substantial ahead of me upon which to tread. Tentatively I extend a foot into the empty darkness but, before it reached the point of fall, a stepping stone immediately appeared beneath it. Likewise with the next step and so forth. And always there was the kind but stern voice saying, 'I shall be behind you all the way, I shall be behind you all the way...' I awoke repeating his words over and over again. At the time I did not fully understand their meaning. I do now. In renewing my contact with the planets, and the Universe in particular, the memories of my own cosmic roots have come flooding back. For many years I had known only the Sun and Danuih as my adopted parents but, as is the case with many adoptees, I have always been fired by a burning desire to discover my real cosmic ancestry. Now I know.

Time Essences do not conform to the hominid gender pattern. As members of the Elemental Kingdoms they are able to function via either positive/active or negative/passive modes as the situation dictates. However, when entering a species which states this requirement, they are obviously obliged to conform, although once the choice is effected they are programmed against deviation. During their sojourn with any species alien to their own kind they are accorded no special privileges, which means they are not exempted from the frailties and sufferings to which all hominids are exposed. In fact, experiencing these adds considerably to their data-banks. However, they do receive a degree of protection which is governed by the specific role they have come to play in the drama of life at the level in question. The hominid experience is particularly painful for them for several reasons, the main two being that due to their basic nature on the one hand, and a feeling of isolation from the 'family group' (which is conducive to melancholia) on the other, they inevitably experience difficulty in conforming to the required norm. Also, being precluded from using their knowledge for any form of material gain or advantage, they may appear ineffectual at the everyday level, and therefore reliant to an extent on minimum assistance from either 'external' sources (their own kind elsewhere in the Universe), or kindly hominids who have become subconsciously (spiritually?) alerted to their needs. End of sad saga!

During my journeys through Time I have been many 'things' and many 'beings', and I shall doubtless be many more before I reach my journey's end. However, once free of the physical vehicle I occupy in this space-time coordinate I shall be reunited with my brethren for a period of order under the aegis of our Father, when we will experience as a group, manifesting as needs demand at any given stage during our eternal journeys through the highways and byways of Time. When chaos once again effects the separation I shall proceed along my own specific Path accompanied, as always, by my faithful feline friend, until such times as I and my brethren are eventually united with the One.


## WITHDRAWAL


But to return to the reality of the present, having reached the advanced age of 66, I feel the time has now come for me to withdraw to a quieter life wherein I can lick my wounds and heal myself. A time to sample, perhaps, some of the gentler aspects of existence in the bosom of Danuih before I finally return this body to the elements who have so kindly loaned me the particles thereof. With the accelerating build-up of chaos on Earth, however, this is not going to be easy. But I think my celestial tutors might see it in their hearts to grant me this short respite. As my readers will have no doubt gathered, life in a hominid body has not been a happy experience for me but, on the credit side, I have made some wonderful friends, the memory of whose kindnesses will remain with me into Eternity, as will my love for them.

This book is, therefore the last of my metaphysical writings. I bequeath it, together with all my others, to those in the present who can grasp its message but mostly to those in the future who will have no difficulty in understanding its content. By then I, and my Time-Essence brethren will be united, rested, and ready to receive our next 'marching orders' from our beloved parent.

May The Timeless Ones be with you.

Endnotes:
(1) Davies, P. *The Mind of God*, p. 34.
(2) Hawking, S. *A Brief History of Time*, pp. 70-73.
(3) Hope, Murry, *Time: The Ultimate Energy*, p. 14.
(4) Lederman, L. M., and Schramm, D. M., *From Quarks to the Cosmos*, p. 161.

# BIBLIOGRAPHY

Bentov, I. *A Cosmic Book*, Inner Traditions International, USA, 1989.

Braghine, A. *The Shadow of Atlantis*, Aquarian Press, London, 1980.

Crossley, Patricia G. *Let's Learn Astrology*, American Federation of Astrologers, Arizona, 1972.

Davies, Paul. *The Mind of God*, Penguin Books, London, 1992.

Dawkins, R. *The Selfish Gene*, Oxford University Press, 1980.

Eliade, M. *Rites and Symbols of Initiation*, Harper & Row, New York, 1975.

George, Demetra. *Asteroid Goddesses*, ASC Publications Inc., San Diego, 1986.

Gribbin, John. *In The Beginning*, Penguin, London, 1993.

Gullan-Whur, M. *The Four Elements*, Century Books, London, 1987.

Hawking, S. *A Brief History of Time*, Bantam Press, 1988.

Hone, M. E. *The Modern Text Book of Astrology*, L. N. Fowler & Co. Ltd., London, 1975.

Hope, M. *The Gaia Dialogues*, Thoth Publications, Loughborough, 1995.

Hope, M. *Atlantis: Myth or Reality?*, Penguin Books, London, 1991.

Hope, M. *Time: The Ultimate Energy*, Element Books, Shaftesbury, 1991.

Hope, M. *The Lion People*, Thoth Publications, Loughborough, 1988.

Hope, M. *The Paschats and the Crystal People*, Thoth Publications, Loughborough, 1992.

Hoyle, Fred. *The Intelligent Universe*, Michael Joseph, London, 1983.

Jung, C. G. *Memories, Dreams & Reflections*, Collins & Routledge & Kegan Paul, London, 1963.

Jung, C. G. *Alchemical Studies*, Routledge & Kegan Paul, London, 1983.

Kerenyi, C. *The Gods of the Greeks*, Thames & Hudson, 1979.

Larousse Encyclopedia of Mythology, Hamlyn, London, 1960.

Lederman, L. M. & Schramm, D. M. *From Quarks to the Cosmos*, Scientific American Library, New York, 1989.

Mead, G. R. S. *Thrice Greatest Hermes*, Theosophical Publishing Co., London, 1906.

Muck, Otto. *The Secrets of Atlantis*, Collins, London, 1978.

Musès, C. *The Lion Path*, Golden Sceptre Publishing, CA, USA, 1985.

Pitt, V. (Ed.). *A Dictionary of Physics*, Penguin, London, 1988.

Readers Digest Association. *Readers Digest Great Illustrated Dictionary*, London, 1985.

Sepharial. *The Manual of Astrology*, Wholesale Book Corporation, New York, 1972.

Sitchin, Z. *Genesis Revisited*, Avon Books, New York, 1990.

Waite, A. E. *The Occult Sciences*, Kegan, Paul, Trench, Trubner & Co. Ltd., London, 1891.

Watson, L. *Gifts of the Unknown*, Destiny Books, Rochester, Vermont, 1991.

Watson, Nancy B. *Practical Solitary Magic*, Samuel Weiser, New York, 1996.

Wolf, Fred Alan. *The Dreaming Universe*, Simon & Schuster, 1994.